CALIFORNIA
KNOWLEDGE, CONCEPTS, AND SKILLS
Every Day for Every Student

- Social Studies Skills Reading and Writing Lessons
- Reading and Note-Taking
- Vocabulary Practice
- Biographies
- Document-Based Question Templates

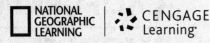

Acknowledgments

Grateful acknowledgment is given to the authors, artists, photographers, museums, publishers, and agents for permission to reprint copyrighted material. Every effort has been made to secure the appropriate permission. If any omissions have been made or if corrections are required, please contact the Publisher.

Photographic Credits

Cover: ©Peter Ptschelinzew/Alamy Stock Photo

Printed in the United States of America

Print Number: 08
Print Year: 2020

For product information and technology assistance, contact us at Customer & Sales Support, 888-915-3276

For permission to use material from this text or product, submit all requests online at **www.cengage.com/permissions**

Further permissions questions can be emailed to **permissionrequest@cengage.com**

National Geographic Learning | Cengage
1 N. State Street, Suite 900
Chicago, IL 60602

Cengage Learning is a leading provider of customized learning solutions with employees residing in nearly 40 different countries and sales in more than 125 countries around the world. Find your local representative at **www.cengage.com.**

Visit National Geographic Learning online at **NGL.Cengage.com/school**

Visit our corporate website at **www.cengage.com**

ISBN: 978-13377-0003-0

WORLD HISTORY KNOWLEDGE AND CONCEPTS

UNIT 1

CHAPTER 1 SECTION 1
The Paleolithic Age

READING AND NOTE-TAKING

SEQUENCE EVENTS

As you read Section 1, use the time line below to keep track of key events in early human history.

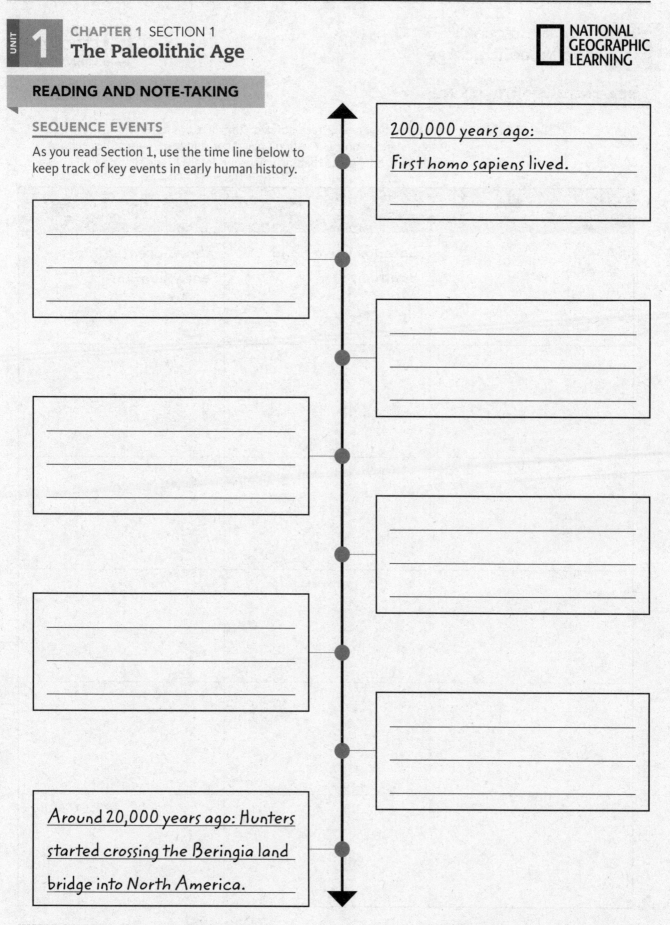

200,000 years ago:

First homo sapiens lived.

Around 20,000 years ago: Hunters started crossing the Beringia land bridge into North America.

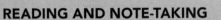

UNIT 1 CHAPTER 1 SECTION 1
The Paleolithic Age

NATIONAL GEOGRAPHIC LEARNING

READING AND NOTE-TAKING

MAKE GENERALIZATIONS Using the chart below, take notes on the different aspects of culture described in Section 1. You don't have to include every aspect of culture mentioned, only those that include other details in the section.

Cultural Activity	Example	Significance
Art	Lascaux Cave hand paintings	shows creativity of early humans

**NATIONAL
GEOGRAPHIC
LEARNING**

READING AND NOTE-TAKING

<u>MAKE CONNECTIONS</u>   After you read Section 2, indicate Hunter-Gatherers **(H)**, Farmers **(F)**, or both **(B)** on the line next to each description below.

___ adapted to new environments

___ lived in favorable climates

___ followed herds of animals

___ developed new weapons that allowed hunting from a distance

___ developed new tools to dig the soil and plant seeds

___ worked together and shared jobs

___ worked in specialized jobs

___ gathered and also started growing plants

___ began taming animals

___ located areas around estuaries to live

___ developed kilns to make clay pots and metal

<u>IDENTIFY MAIN IDEAS AND DETAILS</u>   Use a Main Idea Diagram to organize important information about studying the past featured in Lesson 2.4.

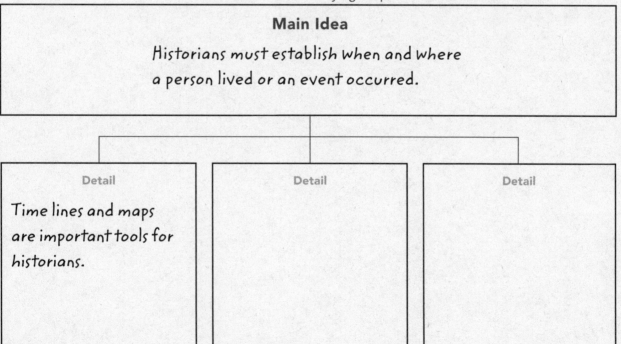

Main Idea

Historians must establish when and where a person lived or an event occurred.

Detail	Detail	Detail
Time lines and maps are important tools for historians.		

UNIT 1

CHAPTER 1 SECTION 2
The Neolithic Age *continued*

READING AND NOTE-TAKING

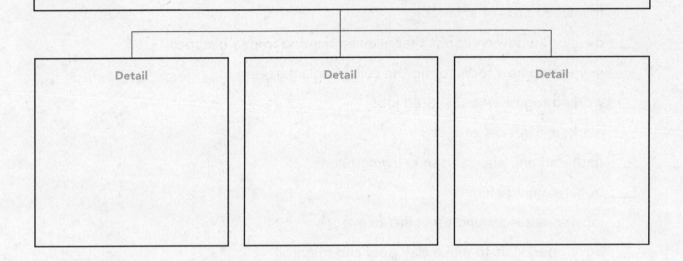

Main Idea

Historians use many different kinds of historical sources to study the past.

Detail	Detail	Detail

Main Idea

Detail	Detail	Detail

UNIT 1

CHAPTER 1 SECTION 1

The Paleolithic Age

NATIONAL GEOGRAPHIC LEARNING

VOCABULARY PRACTICE

KEY VOCABULARY

- **anthropologist** (an-thruh-PAHL-uh-jist) *n.* a scientist who studies the cultural development of humans

- **archaeologist** (ahr-kee-AH-luh-jihst) *n.* a scientist who studies past human life by analyzing fossils and artifacts

- **artifact** (AHR-tih-fakt) *n.* an object made by humans from a past culture

- **culture** *n.* a group's way of life, including types of food, shelter, clothing, language, religion, behavior, and ideas

- **fossil** (FAH-suhl) *n.* the remains of organisms that lived long ago

TOPIC TRIANGLE   Use the Topic Triangle to help you understand the relationships between the Key Vocabulary words. Write at least three sentences about the development of human societies, with the most general description in the top of the diagram and the most specific detail at the bottom. Be sure that your diagram correctly uses all five Key Vocabulary words.

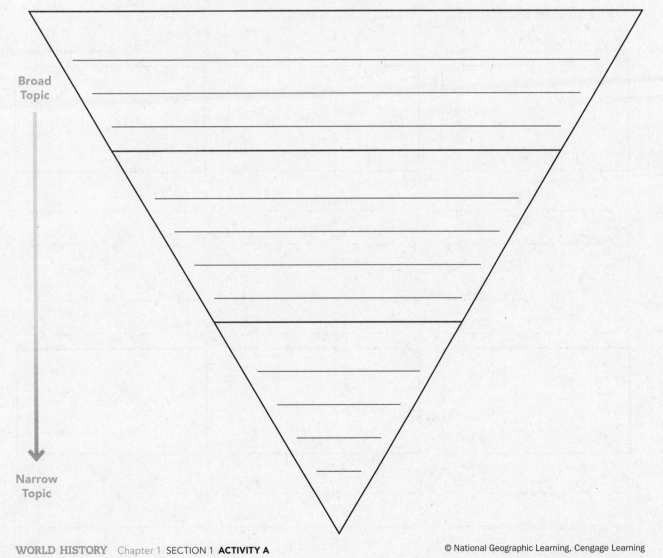

Broad Topic

Narrow Topic

UNIT **1** **CHAPTER 1** SECTION 1
The Paleolithic Age

**NATIONAL
GEOGRAPHIC
LEARNING**

VOCABULARY PRACTICE

KEY VOCABULARY

- **drought** (DROWT) *n.* a long period of dry, hot weather

- **land bridge** *n.* a strip of land connecting two landmasses

- **megafauna** (MEH-guh-faw-nah) *n.* the large animals of a particular region, habitat, or geological period

- **migration** (my-GRAY-shun) *n.* the movement from one place to another

- **oasis** (oh-AY-sihs) *n.* a fertile place with water in a desert

- **technology** (tehk-NAH-loh-gee) *n.* the application of knowledge, tools, and inventions to meet people's needs

PICTURE DICTIONARY Create a dictionary page of words related to the development of human societies. Write each Key Vocabulary word and its definition above the box and then illustrate the word in the box. Then, on the lines below the box, use the word in a sentence.

drought: a long period of
dry, hot weather

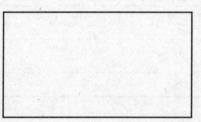

Chapter 1 SECTION 1 **ACTIVITY B** **WORLD HISTORY**

UNIT **1** CHAPTER 1 SECTION 2
The Neolithic Age

NATIONAL
GEOGRAPHIC
LEARNING

VOCABULARY PRACTICE

KEY VOCABULARY

- **agriculture** (a-gruh-KUHL-chur) *n.* the practice of growing plants and rearing animals for food
- **domestication** (doh-mehs-tih-KAY-shun) *n.* the raising of plants and animals to make them useful to humans

- **fertile** (FUHR-tuhl) *adj.* encouraging the growth of crops and plants
- **hunter-gatherer** *n.* a human who hunts animals and gathers wild plants to eat
- **nomad** (NOH-mad) *n.* a person who moves from place to place

CAUSE-AND-EFFECT PARAGRAPH   Write a paragraph explaining the relationship between Neolithic people and the agricultural revolution. Use all five Key Vocabulary words in your paragraph. Begin the paragraph with a clear topic sentence. Then write four to six sentences with supporting details showing cause and effect. Conclude the paragraph with a summarizing sentence.

Topic Sentence:

During the early Paleolithic age people were hunter-gatherers...

_____

_____

_____

_____

_____

_____

_____

_____

_____

Summarizing Sentence:

_____

_____

UNIT 1

CHAPTER 1 SECTION 2
The Neolithic Age

NATIONAL GEOGRAPHIC LEARNING

VOCABULARY PRACTICE

KEY VOCABULARY

- **oral history** *n.* an unwritten account of events, often passed down through the generations as stories or songs

- **primary source** *n.* an artifact or piece of writing that was created by someone who witnessed or lived through a historical event

- **secondary source** *n.* an artifact or writing created after an event by someone who did not see it or live during the time when it occurred

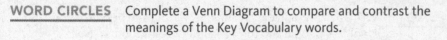

WORD CIRCLES   Complete a Venn Diagram to compare and contrast the meanings of the Key Vocabulary words.

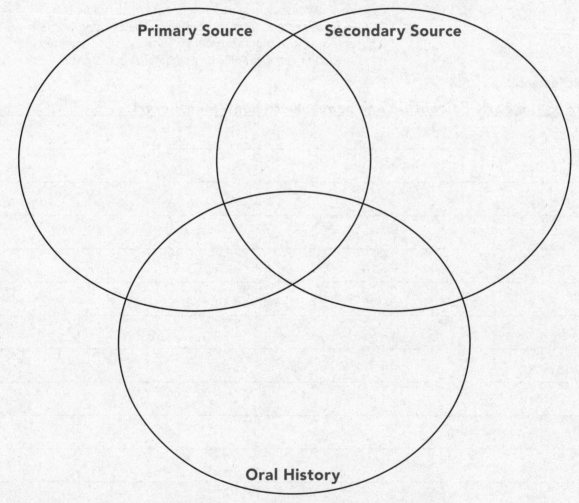

Primary Source   Secondary Source

Oral History

Compare and Contrast   In what ways are historical sources similar and different?

_____

_____

UNIT 1

BIOGRAPHY
RICHARD LEAKEY

The Leakey family name ranks among the most famous in the fields of paleoanthropology and archaeology. Their discoveries in Africa have provided valuable information about the development of humans. True to his family's tradition, Richard Leakey's work in eastern Africa led to the discovery of the earliest fossils of modern humans.

Richard Leakey (1944–)

- **Job:** Paleontologist
- **Passion:** Wildlife Conservation
- **Home:** Kenya

The son of Louis and Mary Leakey, Richard Leakey was born in 1944 in Nairobi, Kenya. As a young boy, Leakey accompanied his parents on many of their field expeditions. However, instead of following in his parents' footsteps, he became a safari guide.

Leakey's career path leading safaris was short lived, though. On a field expedition in 1967, Leakey came upon a site in Koobi Fora in Kenya, along Lake Rudolph (also known as Lake Turkana) where he found several stone tools. From 1967 to 1977, Leakey and his fellow workers uncovered about 400 fossils of early human remains on that site. The finds included tools from the Stone Age dating back 1.9 million years. Koobi Fora became the site of the most diverse set of early human remains found in the world at that time.

Other exciting finds came when Leakey discovered an almost complete 1.6 million-year-old fossil skeleton, which he named "Turkana boy." Leakey also excavated 300 skull fragments that he believed represented the remains of earlier humans who lived in eastern Africa 3.5 million years ago. He wrote about his findings and theories in a book titled *The Making of Mankind*. Leakey also wrote *One Life*, a memoir, in 1983, and a second memoir, *Wildlife Wars: My Fight to Save Africa's Natural Treasures*, in 2001.

Leakey worked in the field as paleontologist, but also in the museum world as the director of the National Museums of Kenya from 1968 to 1989. He became active in the fight against elephant and rhinoceros poaching and for the protection of Kenya's national parks. Leakey also pursued a political career and served in the Kenyan parliament.

Leakey retired from politics in 2001, but he remained active in wildlife conservation. In 2004, he founded WildlifeDirect, a nonprofit conservation organization. This organization raises awareness about endangered species and also connects potential financial donors to various conservation groups.

REVIEW & ASSESS

1. **Draw Conclusions** What led Richard Leakey to pursue a career in archaeology?

_____

_____

2. **Form and Support Opinions** What is Richard Leakey's most important achievement? Support your opinion with details from the reading.

_____

_____

UNIT **1**

BIOGRAPHY

DAME KATHLEEN
KENYON

More than 10,000 years ago, during the Neolithic Age, humans shifted from hunting and gathering to farming for food. Archaeologists have studied this important "event" for many years. Much of what is known about prehistoric and ancient Jericho, located in Southwest Asia, comes from the work of a pathbreaking British archaeologist named Dame Kathleen Kenyon.

Dame Kathleen Kenyon (1906–1978)

- **Job:** Archaeologist
- **Firsts:** First Female President of the Oxford University Archaeological Society
- **Honors:** Named a Dame of the British Empire in 1973

Kathleen Kenyon was born in London, England, in 1906. She studied in England, taught at Oxford University, and became the first female president of the Oxford University Archaeological Society. After graduation, she photographed the excavation of Great Zimbabwe in South Africa. When she returned to England, she joined archaeologist Mortimer Wheeler's excavation team and helped unearth a Roman theater, called the Roman Verulamium, located north of London.

In the following decades, Kenyon worked on many excavations in North Africa and Southwest Asia. She is best known for her discoveries at the site of the prehistoric and ancient settlement of Jericho, a city in the present-day West Bank in Israel. Specifically, she

wanted to determine how the settlement started and how it ended. From 1952 until 1958, Kenyon and her team excavated Jericho and discovered that it dated back to 9000 B.C., making it one of the world's oldest continuously occupied settlements.

While working in Jericho, she developed a new and better method of excavation, now called the "Wheeler-Kenyon method." In this method, instead of peeling off and discarding layer after layer of evidence, archaeologists dig trenches in a checkerboard fashion around an excavation spot. By doing so, they reveal the vertical layers of the site, which helps them understand change over time.

In 1961, Kenyon began excavation work in Jerusalem and continued until 1967. Kenyon wrote about her work in several books, including *Digging Up Jericho*, *Excavations at Jericho*, and *Digging Up Jerusalem*. In 1973, Kenyon was named a Dame of the British Empire. She died in Wales in 1978.

REVIEW & ASSESS

1. **Summarize** What reasons did Kenyon have for excavating the Jericho site?

_____

_____

2. **Make Inferences** What qualities do you think Dame Kenyon most likely possessed to do the work that she did?

_____

_____

READING AND NOTE-TAKING

SUMMARIZE CULTURAL HEARTHS On the first lines below, define *cultural hearth* using your own words. Then, take notes on each of the four cultural hearths as they are introduced in Section 1, using the categories listed in each box.

A cultural hearth is _____

_____

Çatalhöyük

Date: *7400 B.C. (9,000 years ago)* _____

Location: *Southwest Asia* _____

Housing: _____

Food: _____

Religion/Art: _____

Technological Advance: _____

Unusual Fact: _____

_____

Banpo

Date: _____

Location: _____

Housing: _____

Food: _____

Religion/Art: _____

Technological Advance: _____

Unusual Fact: _____

_____

UNIT **1**

CHAPTER 2 SECTION 1
Early Villages *continued*

**NATIONAL
GEOGRAPHIC
LEARNING**

Oaxaca

Date: _____

Location: _____

Housing: _____

Food: _____

Religion/Art: _____

_____

Technological Advance: _____

_____

Unusual Fact: _____

_____

Faiyum

Date: _____

Location: _____

Housing: _____

Food: _____

Religion/Art: _____

_____

Technological Advance: _____

_____

Unusual Fact: _____

_____

UNIT 1

CHAPTER 2 SECTION 2
The Seeds of Civilization

READING AND NOTE-TAKING

CATEGORIZE TRAITS OF CIVILIZATION   Use the table below to define the five key traits of civilization that you read about in Section 2, and then write one example of each.

Trait	Definition	Example
Cities	Large population centers that were centers of cultural, political, and economic development	Ur, one of the busiest cities and trading posts in the ancient world
Complex Institutions		
Specialized Workers		
Record Keeping		
Improved Technology		

UNIT 1

CHAPTER 2 SECTION 2
The Seeds of Civilization

READING AND NOTE-TAKING

FORM AND SUPPORT OPINIONS   As you have read in Lesson 2.1, archaeologists disagree which came first, agriculture or religion. Use the chart below to help you take notes on the development of agriculture and religion as you read Section 2. Then, on the lines below the chart, write a few sentences that state your opinion. Be sure to offer evidence from the section to support why you came to your conclusion.

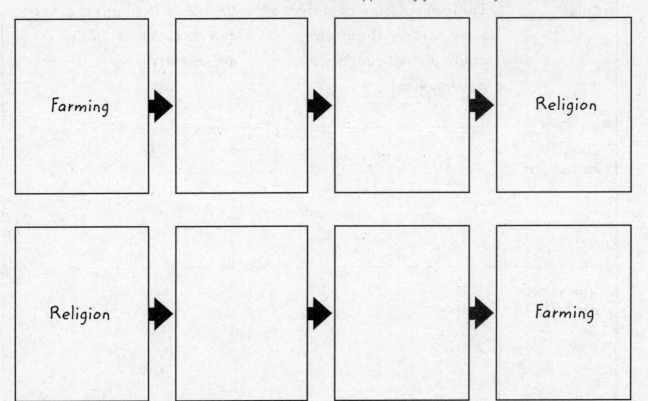

Form and Support Opinions   Which do you think came first, farming or religion?

_____

_____

_____

_____

_____

_____

_____

UNIT 1

CHAPTER 2 SECTION 1
Early Villages

NATIONAL GEOGRAPHIC LEARNING

VOCABULARY PRACTICE

KEY VOCABULARY
- **clan** (KLANN) *n.* a group of families that shares a common ancestor
- **matrilineal** (ma-trah-LIH-nee-uhl) *adj.* relating to descendants traced through the mother

COMPARISON CHART Complete the chart below for both Key Vocabulary words *clan* and *matrilineal*. Write the definition and details for each word, and then explain how the two words are related.

clan	matrilineal

How are these words related?

UNIT 1

CHAPTER 2 SECTION 1
Early Villages

NATIONAL GEOGRAPHIC LEARNING

VOCABULARY PRACTICE

KEY VOCABULARY

- **cultural diffusion** (dih-FEW-zhun) *n.* the process by which cultures interact and ideas spread from one area to another

- **cultural hearth** (HAHRTH) *n.* a place from which new ideas, practices, and technology spread

- **maize** (MAZE) *n.* a type of corn first domesticated by early Mesoamericans

- **metallurgy** (meh-tuhl-UHR-gee) *n.* the science of obtaining metals in their natural form and preparing them for use

- **staple** *n.* a main crop produced in a specific place

- **surplus** (SUHR-plus) *adj.* more than is required or necessary; extra

DEFINITION CHART   Complete a Definition Chart for the Key Vocabulary words.

Word	Definition	In My Own Words
cultural diffusion		

Chapter 2 SECTION 1 **ACTIVITY B**   WORLD HISTORY

UNIT 1 — **CHAPTER 2** SECTION 2
The Seeds of Civilization

NATIONAL GEOGRAPHIC LEARNING

VOCABULARY PRACTICE

KEY VOCABULARY

- **civilization** (sih-vuhl-ih-ZAY-shun) *n.* a society with a highly developed culture and technology

- **religion** (ruh-LIH-juhn) *n.* the belief in and worship of one or more gods and goddesses

- **temple** (TEHM-puhl) *n.* a place of worship

DEFINITION TREE For each Key Vocabulary word in the Definition Tree below, write the definition on the top branch and then use each word in a sentence.

civilization

Definition
a society with a highly developed culture and technology
_____

Sentence
_____
_____

religion

Definition
_____
_____

Sentence
_____
_____

temple

Definition
_____
_____

Sentence
_____
_____

The Seeds of Civilization

VOCABULARY PRACTICE

KEY VOCABULARY

- **city** *n.* a political, economic, and cultural center with a large population
- **government** *n.* an organization set up to make and enforce rules in a society
- **record keeping** *n.* the practice of organizing and storing information
- **scribe** (SKRYB) *n.* a professional writer who recorded official information
- **specialized worker** *n.* a person who performs a job other than farming, such as metalworking or toolmaking
- **trade** *n.* the exchange of goods

EXPOSITORY PARAGRAPH Write a paragraph that explains the traits of civilization. Use all of the Key Vocabulary words. Start with a strong topic sentence, and then write three to six sentences describing the various traits. Be sure to include a summarizing sentence at the end of your paragraph.

Topic Sentence:

_____

_____

_____

_____

_____

_____

_____

_____

_____

_____

Summarizing Sentence:

_____

_____

_____

UNIT 1

BIOGRAPHY
JAMES MELLAART

James Mellaart was a British archaeologist. He is most famous for his discovery of and excavations at Çatalhöyük, a Neolithic settlement in present-day Turkey.

- **Job:** Archaeologist
- **Lucky Break:** Job at the National Museum of Antiquities in Leiden, Netherlands
- **Discovery:** Çatalhöyük

James Mellaart was born in London, England, in 1925, to a Dutch-born father who was an art expert and a Northern Irish mother. In 1932, because of economic hard times, Mellaart's family moved to the Netherlands.

During World War II, when Mellaart was just 15 years old, the Nazis called on him to serve in the German army. Instead, his father sent him away to work at the National Museum of Antiquities in the Dutch city of Leiden. This decision changed Mellaart's life. Surrounded by ancient artifacts, he became fascinated by the ancient world.

After the war, he studied archaeology at the University College of London and graduated in 1951. Soon after graduation, as a research grantee of the British Institute of Archaeology, Mellaart began exploring vast areas of southern Anatolia in Turkey. There, he uncovered several unknown sites, including the one for which he is most famous: Çatalhöyük.

From 1961 to 1965, Mellaart oversaw excavations at Çatalhöyük, which archaeologists think might be the world's first city and the oldest known permanent

James Mellaart (1925–2012)

settlement. Çatalhöyük might have housed as many as 10,000 people. Mellaart's team unearthed about 200 flat-roofed mud-brick houses and other exciting finds. They discovered dome-shaped clay ovens and roof holes that were likely used as doors for people to enter and exit the dwellings. The team determined that the skeletons that they discovered were ceremonially buried. They also excavated axes and knives, as well as figures of female goddesses. All of these findings demonstrated that Çatalhöyük was the center of an advanced culture.

Mellaart's discoveries at Çatalhöyük also showed that Anatolia was an important area in the development of Neolithic people. Çatalhöyük continues to be an accessible archaeological site. James Mellaart died in London, England, in July 2012.

REVIEW & ASSESS

1. **Summarize** What sparked James Mellaart's interest in archaeology?

_____

_____

2. **Make Inferences** Why do you think the work and findings of archaeologists such as James Mellaart are important?

_____

_____

UNIT **2** **CHAPTER 3** SECTION 1
Sumer

NATIONAL
GEOGRAPHIC
LEARNING

READING AND NOTE-TAKING

SEQUENCE EVENTS   As you read Section 1, complete this Sequence Chain with details about how civilization developed in Mesopotamia. Use the section's headings and subheadings as a guide.

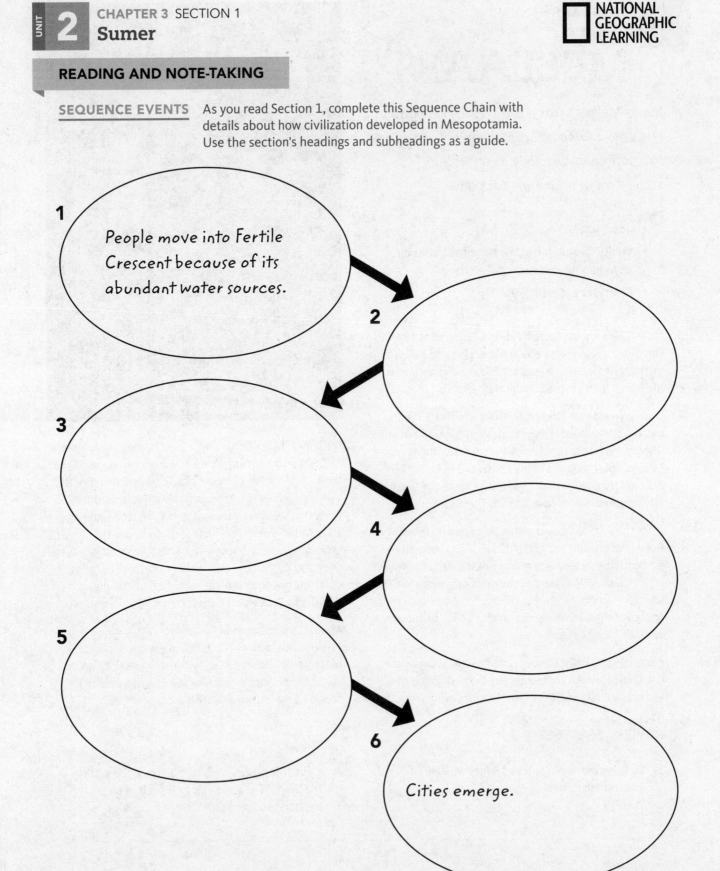

1 People move into Fertile Crescent because of its abundant water sources.

2

3

4

5

6 Cities emerge.

UNIT 2   **CHAPTER 3** SECTION 1
Sumer *continued*

NATIONAL
GEOGRAPHIC
LEARNING

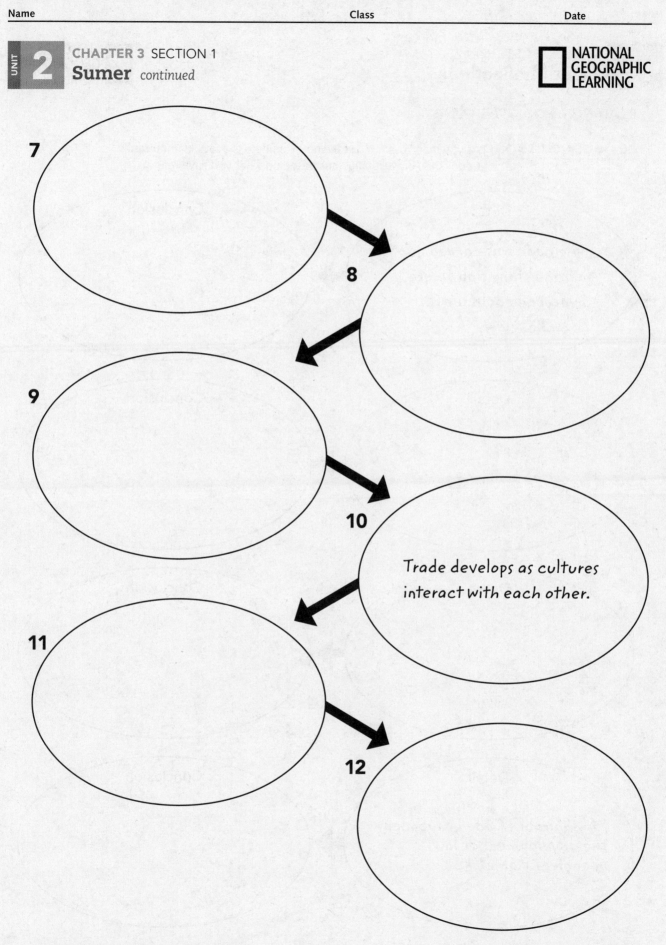

7

8

9

10

Trade develops as cultures interact with each other.

11

12

Chapter 3 SECTION 1 **ACTIVITY A**   WORLD HISTORY

UNIT **2** **CHAPTER 3** SECTION 2
Later Civilizations

NATIONAL GEOGRAPHIC LEARNING

READING AND NOTE-TAKING

DRAW CONCLUSIONS As you read Lesson 2.1, take notes on details about Hammurabi's Code. Then draw conclusions based on what you have read.

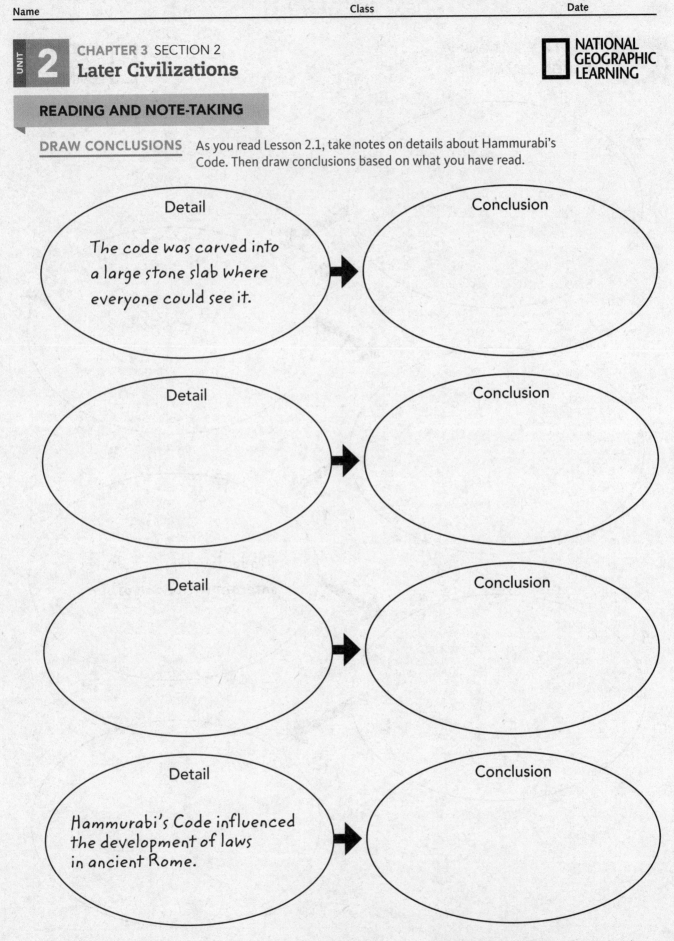

Detail

The code was carved into a large stone slab where everyone could see it.

Conclusion

Detail

Conclusion

Detail

Conclusion

Detail

Hammurabi's Code influenced the development of laws in ancient Rome.

Conclusion

UNIT **2** CHAPTER 3 SECTION 2
Later Civilizations

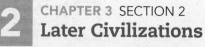

READING AND NOTE-TAKING

<u>ORGANIZE INFORMATION</u> Use a chart to organize information about
civilizations described in Section 2.

Civilization	Characteristics	Best Known For
Babylonians		Hammurabi's Code of Laws

Chapter 3 SECTION 2 **ACTIVITY B** WORLD HISTORY

UNIT 2

CHAPTER 3 SECTION 1
Sumer

NATIONAL GEOGRAPHIC LEARNING

VOCABULARY PRACTICE

KEY VOCABULARY

- **artisan** (AHR-tih-zun) *n.* a person skilled at making things by hand
- **city-state** *n.* a self-governing unit made up of a city and its surrounding lands and settlements; a city that controls the surrounding villages and towns
- **irrigation** (ihr-uh-GAY-shuhn) *n.* the supply of water to fields using human-made systems
- **silt** (SIHLT) *n.* an especially fine and fertile soil
- **social class** *n.* a category of people based on wealth or status in a society

DESCRIPTIVE PARAGRAPH   Using each of the five Key Vocabulary words, write a paragraph describing how adapting to the physical geography, developing new farming techniques, and producing agricultural surpluses led to the establishment of city-states in the Fertile Crescent. Be sure to write a clear topic sentence as your first sentence. Then write at least four to six sentences with supporting details. Conclude your paragraph with a summarizing sentence.

Topic Sentence:

_____

_____

_____

_____

_____

_____

_____

_____

Summarizing Sentence:

_____

_____

_____

© National Geographic Learning, Cengage Learning

UNIT 2

CHAPTER 3 SECTION 1
Sumer

NATIONAL GEOGRAPHIC LEARNING

VOCABULARY PRACTICE

KEY VOCABULARY

- **cuneiform** (kyoo-NEE-uh-fawrm) *n.* the earliest form of writing, invented by the Sumerians

- **empire** (EHM-pyre) *n.* a group of different lands and people governed by one ruler

- **famine** (FAM-uhn) *n.* an extreme lack of crops or food causing widespread hunger

- **polytheism** (pahl-ee-THEE-iz-uhm) *n.* a belief in many gods

- **ritual** (RIH-choo-uhl) *n.* a formal series of acts always performed in the same way; a religious ceremony

- **tribute** (TRIH-byoot) *n.* a tax paid or goods and services rendered in return for protection

- **ziggurat** (ZIH-guh-raht) *n.* a pyramid-shaped temple in a Sumerian city-state

THREE-COLUMN CHART Complete the chart for each of the seven Key Vocabulary words. Write each word's definition, and then provide a definition in your own words.

Word	Definition	In My Own Words
cuneiform	the earliest form of writing, invented by the Sumerians	a writing system the Sumerians invented

Chapter 3 SECTION 1 **ACTIVITY B** WORLD HISTORY

NATIONAL GEOGRAPHIC LEARNING

VOCABULARY PRACTICE

KEY VOCABULARY

- **province** (PRAH-vinhs) *n.* an administrative district of a larger empire or country
- **satrap** (SAY-trap) *n.* a governor of a province in the Persian Empire
- **tolerance** (TAHL-uhr-uhns) *n.* the sympathy for the beliefs and practices of others

TOPIC TRIANGLE   Use the Topic Triangle to help you understand the relationship between the Key Vocabulary words. Write several sentences about how Cyrus the Great and Darius I ruled and expanded the Persian Empire. Begin with a sentence using *tolerance* at the top of the triangle. Then write a sentence using *province* in the middle and *satrap* at the bottom. Be sure that your diagram correctly uses all of the Key Vocabulary words.

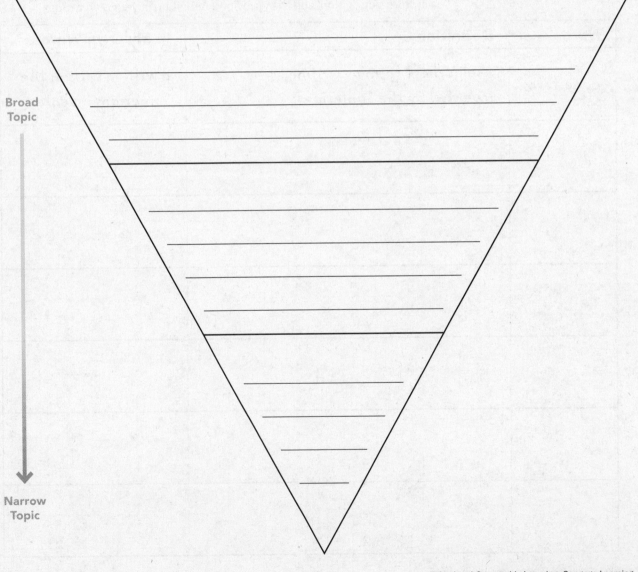

Broad Topic

Narrow Topic

© National Geographic Learning, Cengage Learning

UNIT **2**   **CHAPTER 3** SECTION 2
Later Civilizations

NATIONAL GEOGRAPHIC LEARNING

VOCABULARY PRACTICE

KEY VOCABULARY

- **alliance** (uh-LY-uhns) *n.* an agreement between nations to fight each other's enemies; a partnership
- **colony** (KAHL-uh-nee) *n.* a group of people that settles in a new land but keeps ties to its native country

- **legacy** (LEH-guh-see) *n.* the things, both cultural and technological, left to us from past cultures
- **raw material** *n.* a substance from which other things are made

__WDS CHART__   Complete a Word-Definition-Sentence (WDS) Chart for each Key Vocabulary word.

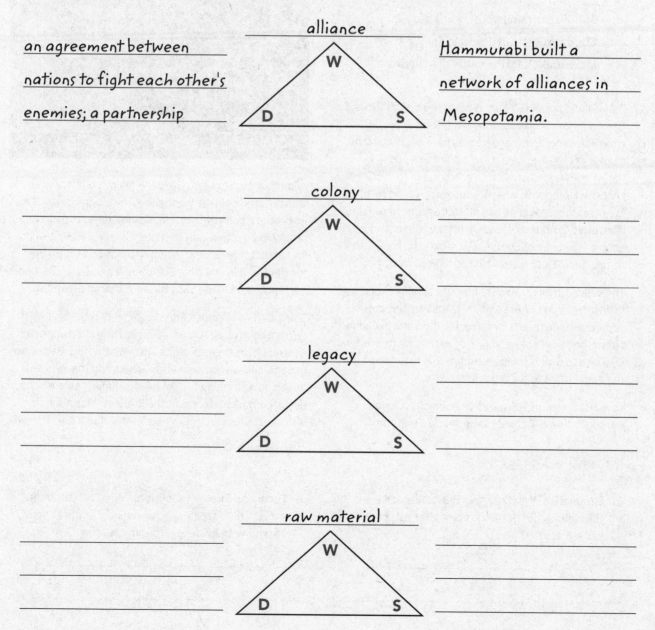

alliance

W

D   S

an agreement between nations to fight each other's enemies; a partnership

Hammurabi built a network of alliances in Mesopotamia.

colony

W

D   S

legacy

W

D   S

raw material

W

D   S

Chapter 3 SECTION 2 **ACTIVITY B**   WORLD HISTORY

UNIT 2

BIOGRAPHY

DARIUS I

Darius I was one of the most powerful rulers of the ancient world. He ruled the Persian Empire at its height, from 522 to 486 B.C. Some of what is known about Darius's rule comes from his own inscriptions on the side of a rocky cliff in ancient Persia, now part of present-day Iran.

- **Job:** Persian Emperor
- **Triumph:** Expanded Persian Empire
- **Downfall:** Defeat at Battle of Marathon

Relief sculpture of Darius I (550 B.C.–486 B.C.)

Darius I was born in 550 B.C. during the reign of Cyrus the Great. His father Hystaspes was a satrap, or provincial governor, under Cyrus and he may have been a distant relative of the king. Because of his father's position, Darius grew up in Cyrus's court. According to the Greek historian Herodotus, when Darius was a young man, Cyrus suspected that he had plotted against him. Years later, after Cyrus died, Darius, with the help of six Persian nobles, killed one of Cyrus's sons, who was the heir to the throne. In 522 B.C., he established himself as king.

The sudden change of rulers brought about revolts in different parts of the empire. Darius and his army suppressed the revolts by force. He then proceeded to strengthen the Persian Empire by extending its borders. By 519 B.C., Darius ruled an empire that extended from the Aegean Sea to the Indus River.

To maintain control of such a large empire, Darius introduced several changes. He set up a uniform system of government, fixed the tax rates, introduced standardized coinage throughout the empire, and instituted a code of laws. He promoted trade by dredging up an old Egyptian canal between the Nile River and the Red Sea. Darius built a system of roads and set up inns for travelers. In addition, Darius built palaces at Susa and Persepolis and made Susa the administrative capital.

Some parts of Darius's empire began to rebel against Persian control. In 500 B.C., Greek city-states supported the Ionians in their revolt against Persian rule. Darius was furious, and war between the Greeks and the Persians began. In a stunning turn of events, the Athenians defeated Darius's forces at the Battle of Marathon in 490 B.C. Darius died four years later in 486 B.C.

REVIEW & ASSESS

1. **Summarize** What changes did Darius make throughout the Persian Empire after establishing himself as king?

2. **Form and Support Opinions** What do you think was Darius's greatest achievement? Support your answer with evidence from the reading.

_____

_____

DOCUMENT-BASED QUESTION

Use the questions here to help you analyze the sources and write your paragraph.

DOCUMENT ONE: Cuneiform Tablet, Northern Iraq, c. 600s B.C.

1A How would you describe this artifact?

_____

_____

1B **Constructed Response** Why did the Sumerians dry the clay cuneiform tablets?

_____

_____

DOCUMENT TWO: from *The Epic of Gilgamesh*

2A What is the main point of this passage from *Gilgamesh*?

_____

_____

2B **Constructed Response** Why would the Sumerians record a story about their king encountering a monster?

_____

DOCUMENT THREE: from *The Epic of Creation*

3A How would you summarize this part of the epic in your own words?

_____

_____

3B **Constructed Response** Why might Babylonians want to tell and record their story of the creation of the world?

_____

SYNTHESIZE & WRITE

What did the Sumerians' cuneiform writing system make possible?

Topic Sentence: _____

_____

Your Paragraph: _____

_____

_____

_____

UNIT **2**

CHAPTER 4 SECTION 1
A Society on the Nile

**NATIONAL
GEOGRAPHIC
LEARNING**

READING AND NOTE-TAKING

SUMMARIZE DETAILS   As you read Section 1, keep track of details in the text in a Summary Diagram. Then, summarize the development of civilization in the Nile River Delta in a few sentences in the box provided below.

Facts

Facts

Facts

Setting

Nile River

Summary

UNIT 2 — CHAPTER 4 SECTION 1
A Society on the Nile

NATIONAL
GEOGRAPHIC
LEARNING

READING AND NOTE-TAKING

COMPARE AND CONTRAST Use a Venn Diagram to compare and contrast how government and religion overlapped and diverged in ancient Egypt. Then answer the question below.

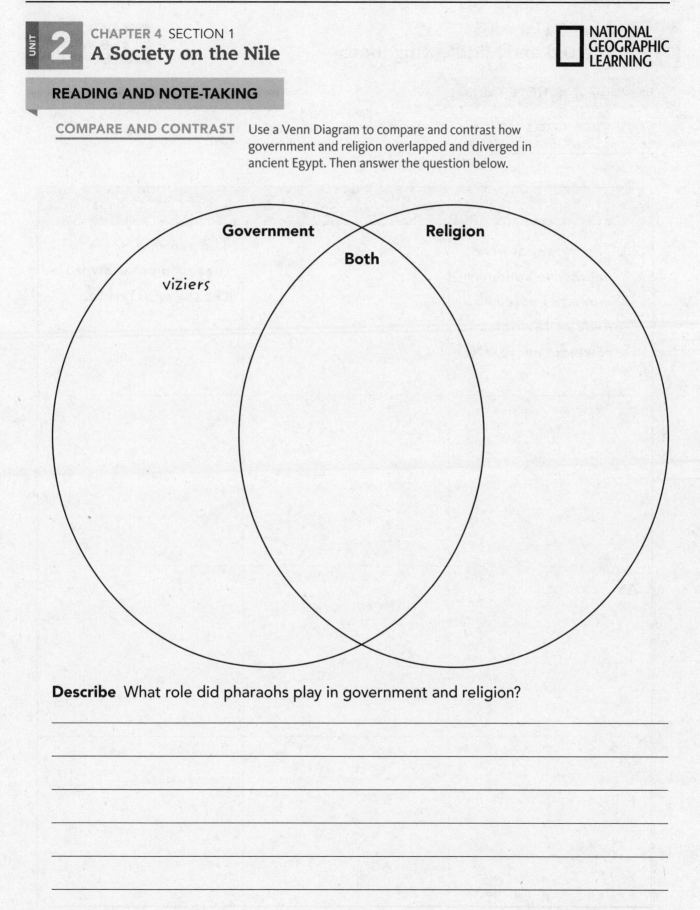

Government

Religion

Both

viziers

Describe What role did pharaohs play in government and religion?

_____

_____

_____

_____

_____

_____

READING AND NOTE-TAKING

SYNTHESIZE VISUAL AND TEXTUAL INFORMATION Use a Three-Column Chart to record the textual and visual information and supporting details from each lesson of Section 2.

Textual Information	Visual Information	Supporting Details
2.1 The Pyramids were impressive buildings made to house the dead of the rich and powerful of society.		The pyramids seem to suggest a path toward the sky or afterlife.
2.2		
2.3		
2.4		

The Old and Middle Kingdoms

READING AND NOTE-TAKING

CATEGORIZE INFORMATION   Use the boxes below to categorize information about the Old Kingdom, the Middle Kingdom, and religion and daily life in ancient Egypt as you read Section 2.

Old Kingdom

- 2700–2200 B.C.
- first period of unity and wealth

Middle Kingdom

Religion and Daily life

Chapter 4 SECTION 2 **ACTIVITY B**   WORLD HISTORY

UNIT **2** CHAPTER 4 SECTION 3
The New Kingdom

NATIONAL
GEOGRAPHIC
LEARNING

READING AND NOTE-TAKING

SEQUENCE EVENTS As you read Section 3, take note of major events in the lives and reigns of Hatshepsut and Ramses.

Hatshepsut

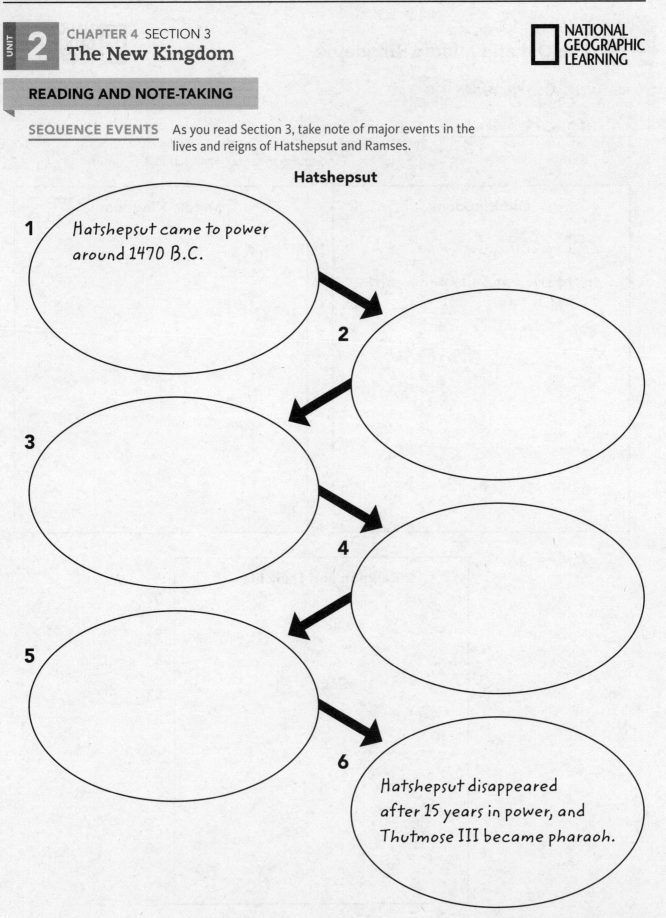

1 Hatshepsut came to power around 1470 B.C.

2

3

4

5

6 Hatshepsut disappeared after 15 years in power, and Thutmose III became pharaoh.

Ramses

1 Early in his reign, Ramses expanded the empire into Nubia, Libya, and the eastern Mediterranean.

2

3

4

5

6 After Ramses's death, Egypt lost power and was conquered by foreign powers.

UNIT **2**

CHAPTER 4 SECTION 4
The Egyptian Legacy

NATIONAL
GEOGRAPHIC
LEARNING

READING AND NOTE-TAKING

CATEGORIZE INFORMATION   As you read Section 4, complete a Concept Cluster to categorize information about different aspects of ancient Egypt's legacy.

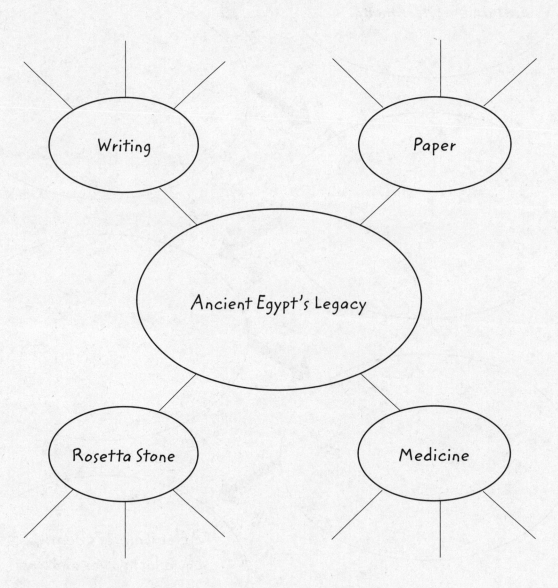

© National Geographic Learning, Cengage Learning

NATIONAL GEOGRAPHIC LEARNING

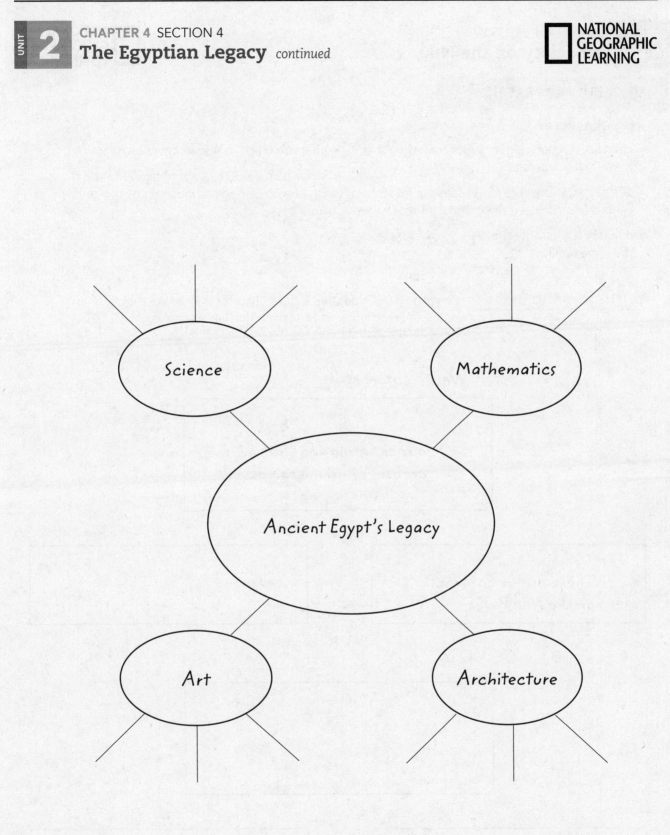

UNIT **2** **CHAPTER 4** SECTION 1
A Society on the Nile

NATIONAL GEOGRAPHIC LEARNING

VOCABULARY PRACTICE

KEY VOCABULARY

- **cataract** (CAT-uh-rakt) *n.* a rock formation that creates churning rapids
- **delta** *n.* an area where a river fans out into various branches as it flows into a body of water
- **dynasty** (DY-nuh-stee) *n.* a series of rulers from the same family
- **pharaoh** (FEHR-oh) *n.* an Egyptian ruler
- **vizier** (vuh-ZEER) *n.* a chief official in ancient Egypt who carried out much of the day-to-day work of governing

DEFINITION AND DETAILS Complete a Definition and Details Chart for the Key Vocabulary words. For each word, write its definition and examples or other details related to the word from the section.

Word: <u>cataract</u>

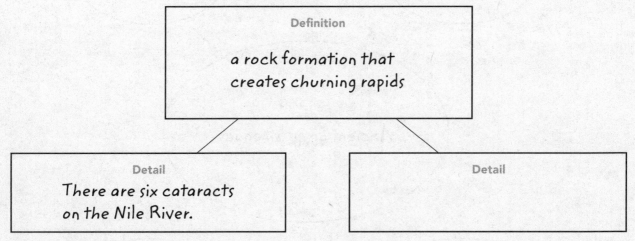

Definition

a rock formation that creates churning rapids

Detail

There are six cataracts on the Nile River.

Detail

Word: _____

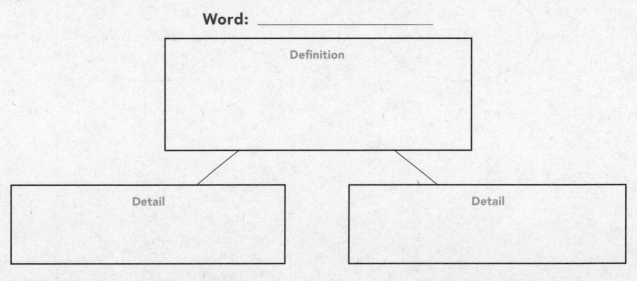

Definition

Detail

Detail

A Society on the Nile *continued*

NATIONAL GEOGRAPHIC LEARNING

Word: ____________________

Definition

Detail

Detail

Word: ____________________

Definition

Detail

Detail

Word: ____________________

Definition

Detail

Detail

UNIT 2

CHAPTER 4 SECTION 2
The Old and Middle Kingdoms

**NATIONAL
GEOGRAPHIC
LEARNING**

VOCABULARY PRACTICE

KEY VOCABULARY

- **hierarchy** (HY-rar-kee)) *n.* a system in which people belong to different social classes that have different ranks in society

- **mummy** *n.* the preserved body of a pharaoh or other powerful person in ancient Egypt

- **pyramid** (PEER-uh-mihd) *n.* a massive monumental tomb for a pharaoh

<u>**WORDS IN CONTEXT**</u>   Follow the directions for using the Key Vocabulary words in context.

1. Explain why *pyramids* were built.

_____

_____

_____

_____

_____

_____

2. Describe the *hierarchy* of society in ancient Egypt.

_____

_____

_____

_____

_____

_____

3. Explain how *mummies* were made.

_____

_____

_____

_____

_____

_____

The Old and Middle Kingdoms

VOCABULARY PRACTICE

KEY VOCABULARY

- **hierarchy** (HY-rar-kee) *n.* a system in which people belong to social classes of different ranks

- **mummy** *n.* the preserved body of a pharaoh or other powerful person in ancient Egypt

- **pyramid** (PEER-uh-mihd) *n.* a massive monumental tomb for a pharaoh

TRAVEL ARTICLE Imagine you are a travel writer visiting modern Egypt. Use details from Section 2 to describe your experiences exploring pyramids, viewing mummies in museums, and learning about the social structure and hierarchy of ancient Egyptian society. Use all of the Key Vocabulary words in your article.

Article Title: _____

Date: _____

_____

_____

_____

_____

_____

_____

_____

_____

_____

_____

_____

_____

_____

UNIT 2

CHAPTER 4 SECTION 3
The New Kingdom

VOCABULARY PRACTICE

KEY VOCABULARY
- **barter** (BAHR-tuhr) *v.* to exchange goods

VOCABULARY PYRAMID   Complete a Vocabulary Pyramid for the Key Vocabulary word *barter*.

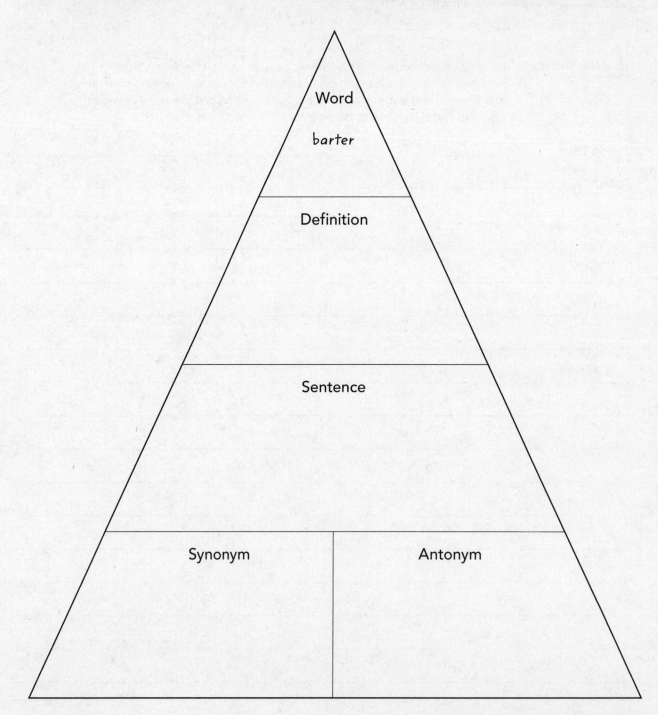

Word

barter

Definition

Sentence

Synonym   Antonym

UNIT 2

CHAPTER 4 SECTION 3
The New Kingdom

NATIONAL
GEOGRAPHIC
LEARNING

VOCABULARY PRACTICE

KEY VOCABULARY

- **barter** (BAHR-tuhr) *v.* to exchange goods

DEFINITION CHART Complete a Three-Column Chart for the Key Vocabulary word.
Then illustrate the word *barter* in the bottom box.

Word	Definition	In My Own Words

Vocabulary Illustration

UNIT 2

CHAPTER 4 SECTION 4

The Egyptian Legacy

NATIONAL
GEOGRAPHIC
LEARNING

VOCABULARY PRACTICE

KEY VOCABULARY

- **hieroglyph** (HY-ruh-glihf) *n.* a picture representing an object, sound, or idea that was part of the ancient Egyptian writing system

- **papyrus** (puh-PY-ruhs) *n.* a paperlike material made from reeds

- **scribe** (SCRYB) *n.* a professional writer who recorded official information

RELATED IDEA WEB Write each of the Key Vocabulary words inside a circle, along with its definition in your own words. Then draw lines or arrows connecting the circles to show how the words are related, based on what you read in Section 4. Write your explanation of the connection next to the line or arrow.

hieroglyph

UNIT 2 | CHAPTER 4 SECTION 4
The Egyptian Legacy

NATIONAL GEOGRAPHIC LEARNING

VOCABULARY PRACTICE

KEY VOCABULARY

- **hieroglyph** (HY-ruh-glihf) *n.* a picture representing an object, sound, or idea that was part of the ancient Egyptian writing system

- **papyrus** (puh-PY-ruhs) *n.* a paperlike material made from reeds

- **scribe** (SCRYB) *n.* a professional writer who recorded official information

DEFINITION CHART   Complete a Definition Chart for the Key Vocabulary words.

Word	hieroglyph	papyrus	scribe
Definition			
In Your Own Words			
Symbol or Diagram			

Chapter 4 SECTION 4 **ACTIVITY B**   WORLD HISTORY

UNIT 2

BIOGRAPHY
HATSHEPSUT

Hatshepsut was an ancient Egyptian ruler. She was, in fact, a female king. Her reign lasted about 15 years, from 1473 to 1458 B.C. She oversaw a mostly peaceful time, focusing her foreign policy on trade and building projects.

- **Job:** Egyptian King
- **Goal:** Expanding Trade
- **Monument:** Temple at Dayr al-Bahri

Hatshepsut (1508 B.C.–1458 B.C.) portrayed as a sphinx, with a man's beard

Kenneth Garrett/National Geographic Creative

Hatshepsut (hat-SHEP-suht), the daughter of King Thutmose I, was born in 1508 B.C. As was the Egyptian custom, Hatshepsut married her half brother Thutmose II, who became king in 1491 B.C., after Thutmose I died. After the death of Thutmose II, her stepson, Thutmose III, became king. However, because he was still a baby, Hatshepsut ruled as regent.

After about seven years, Hatshepsut was viewed not only as co-ruler with Thutmose III, but as the dominant king. At first, Hatshepsut's portraits showed her as queen with a female body and female clothes. Eventually her formal portraits began to show her with a male body and male clothes. No one knows for sure how Hatshepsut managed to persuade Egyptian leaders to accept her as king. Hatshepsut surrounded herself with officials she chose and who would be loyal to her.

Hatshepsut's period of rule was generally peaceful, though she did order a military campaign in Nubia. One of the hallmarks of her reign was the expansion of trade.

Scenes on a wall of her temple show an expedition to Punt, a center of trade, which brought back goods such as gold, wood, animal skins, and myrrh trees. Hatshepsut is also known for her extensive building programs. In Thebes, she built a temple to the god Amon-Re, as well as other temples and obelisks throughout Egypt. Hatshepsut's biggest achievement was her Dayr al-Bahri temple, built as a monument to herself.

In time, Hatshepsut allowed Thutmose III to play a more significant role in government affairs. After she died, Thutmose ruled Egypt for more than 33 years. Concerned about his own position and power, Thutmose tried to erase all traces of his stepmother, Hatshepsut, as king. He had her statues torn down and had her name removed from an official list of rulers. Historians believe Thutmose III wanted to demonstrate that the succession of Egyptian kings ran from Thutmose I to Thutmose II to Thutmose III—and not through Hatshepsut, the king.

REVIEW & ASSESS

1. **Draw Conclusions** Why did Hatshepsut surround herself with officials that she had chosen?

_____

_____

2. **Make Inferences** Why do you think Hatshepsut showed herself as having a male body and wearing men's clothes in her portraits?

_____

_____

UNIT 2

CHAPTER 4 LESSON 2.3
Life, Death, and Religion

NATIONAL GEOGRAPHIC LEARNING

DOCUMENT-BASED QUESTION

Use the questions here to help you analyze the sources and write your paragraph.

DOCUMENT ONE: from *Hymn to the Nile*, c. 2100 B.C.

1A What does this poem tell you about the Nile?

_____

_____

1B Constructed Response Why might ancient Egyptians have wanted to praise the Nile River each year by reciting this religious poem?

_____

_____

DOCUMENT TWO: from the *Book of the Dead*

2A Restate the main point of this text in your own words.

_____

_____

2B Constructed Response What does this passage suggest about Re's role in ancient Egyptian beliefs?

_____

_____

DOCUMENT THREE: Sun God Re in Falcon Form, Ancient Egypt

3A How would you describe this artifact?

_____

_____

3B Constructed Response What can you infer about Re's connection to nature from his representation in this statue?

_____

_____

SYNTHESIZE & WRITE

What did the Egyptians believe about their gods' control of their world?

Topic Sentence: _____

_____

Your Paragraph: _____

_____

_____

_____

_____

UNIT 2

CHAPTER 5 SECTION 1
The Founding of Judaism

READING AND NOTE-TAKING

SYNTHESIZE VISUAL AND TEXTUAL INFORMATION After you read Section 1, use the visual and textual information from the section as well as the map in Lesson 1.1 to answer the questions below.

1. What is the title of the map? _____

_____

_____

2. What does the red line on the map represent? _____

_____

_____

_____

3. What does the green line on the map represent? _____

_____

_____

_____

4. What is the significance of Mount Sinai? _____

_____

_____

_____

5. If the Hebrews left Egypt for Canaan and arrived in 1250 B.C., and the journey took 40 years, when did they leave Egypt? _____

_____

_____

_____

UNIT 2 — CHAPTER 5 SECTION 1
The Founding of Judaism

READING AND NOTE-TAKING

IDENTIFY SIGNIFICANCE   As you read Section 1, take notes about the actions of historical figures mentioned in the text. Then, in the third column, identify why each historical figure's actions are significant.

Historical Figure	Actions	Significance
Abraham	Brought his people to live in Canaan	

UNIT 2 **CHAPTER 5** SECTION 2
Kingdoms and Exile

NATIONAL GEOGRAPHIC LEARNING

READING AND NOTE-TAKING

OUTLINE AND TAKE NOTES As you read Section 2, take notes using the headings and subheadings of Lessons 2.1–2.3, as a starting point. Then write a few sentences to summarize the content.

2.1 Israel and Judah

A. _Line of Kings_

- _King Saul protected his people from the Philistines._

- _____

- _____

- _____

B. _Invaded and Conquered_

- _____

- _____

- _____

- _____

2.2 Exile and Return

A. _____

- _____

- _____

- _____

- _____

B. _____

- _____

- _____

- _____

- _____

© National Geographic Learning, Cengage Learning

2.3 The Diaspora

A. _____

- _____

- _____

- _____

- _____

B. _____

- _____

- _____

- _____

- _____

Summary: _____

_____

_____

_____

_____

_____

_____

_____

_____

_____

_____

_____

UNIT **2**
CHAPTER 5 SECTION 1
The Founding of Judaism

**NATIONAL
GEOGRAPHIC
LEARNING**

VOCABULARY PRACTICE

KEY VOCABULARY

- **covenant** (KUHV-uh-nuhnt) *n.* a religious agreement
- **monotheism** (mah-noh-THEE-izm) *n.* the worship of a single God

CAUSE-AND-EFFECT CHART Define the Key Vocabulary words *monotheism* and *covenant*. Use the chart to explain how the Hebrew covenant was the result of monotheism.

Causes

monotheism: the worship of a
single God

_____

_____

_____

_____

_____

_____

_____

_____

_____

_____

_____

_____

_____

Effects

covenant: _____

_____

_____

_____

_____

_____

_____

_____

_____

_____

_____

_____

_____

_____

_____

_____

_____

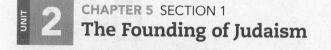

UNIT 2 — CHAPTER 5 SECTION 1
The Founding of Judaism

NATIONAL GEOGRAPHIC LEARNING

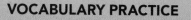

VOCABULARY PRACTICE

KEY VOCABULARY

- **confederation** (kuhn-fehd-uh-RAY-shun) *n.* a group of allies
- **kosher** (KOH-shuhr) *adj.* specially prepared according to Jewish dietary laws
- **rabbi** (RAHB-eye) *n.* a Jewish spiritual leader
- **synagogue** (SIHN-uh-gahg) *n.* a Jewish place of worship
- **tribe** (TRYB) *n.* an extended family unit

KWL CHART   Fill in the KWL Chart for the Key Vocabulary words.

Word	What I Know	What I Want to Know	What I Learned
confederation			

CHAPTER 5 SECTION 2
Kingdoms and Exile

VOCABULARY PRACTICE

KEY VOCABULARY

- **exile** (EHK-zile) *n.* the forced removal from one's native country

WORD WHEEL   Follow the instructions below to analyze the Key Vocabulary word *exile*.

1. Write the word in the center of the wheel.

2. Look in your textbook for examples of descriptions related to the word, or think of any related words you already know.

3. Write your descriptions and related words on the spokes of the wheel. Add more spokes if needed.

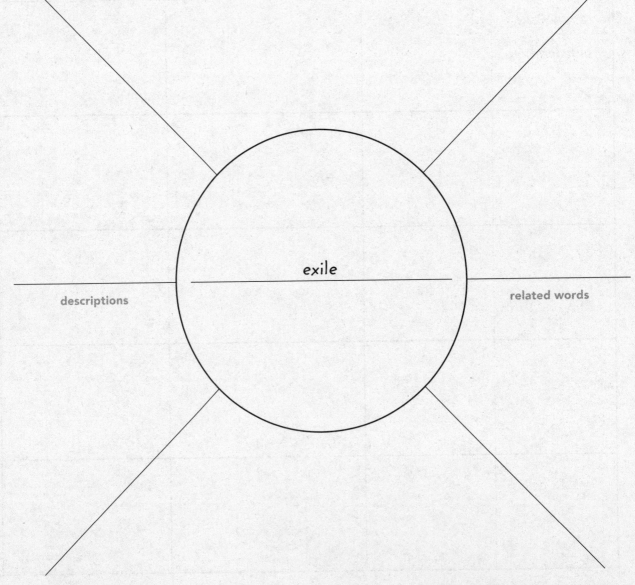

exile

descriptions   related words

UNIT 2 CHAPTER 5 SECTION 2
Kingdoms and Exile

NATIONAL GEOGRAPHIC LEARNING

VOCABULARY PRACTICE

KEY VOCABULARY

- **exile** (EHK-zile) *n.* the forced removal from one's native country

WORD SQUARE   Complete a Word Square for the Key Vocabulary word *exile*.

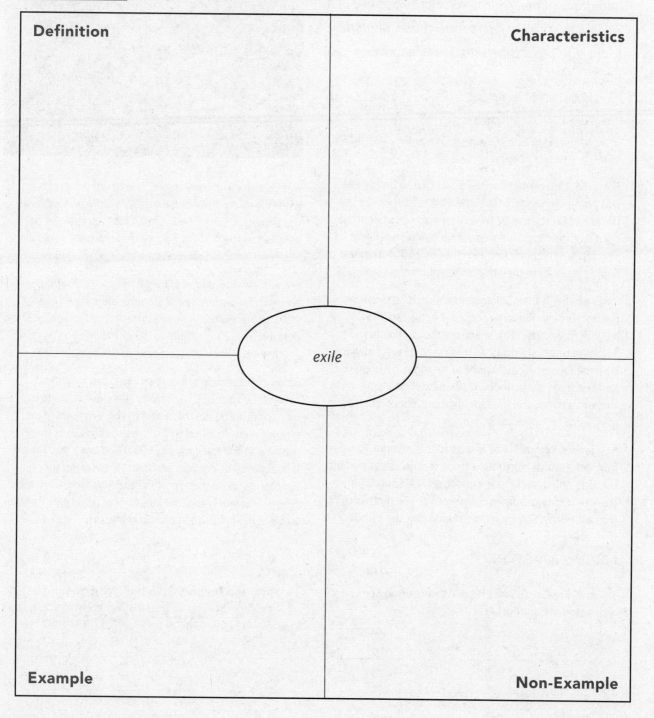

Definition

Characteristics

exile

Example

Non-Example

Chapter 5 SECTION 2 **ACTIVITY B**   **WORLD HISTORY**

Fine Art Images/Heritage Image Partnership Ltd/Alamy

UNIT 2

BIOGRAPHY
SOLOMON

Solomon is considered one of the greatest kings of the ancient Israelites. Much of what is known about him comes from writings in the Hebrew Bible. During his rule, Israel became an important commercial power. However, some of Solomon's decisions led to conflict and, ultimately, to the division of Israel into two kingdoms.

- **Job:** King of Israel
- **Skill:** Solving Disputes
- **Virtues:** Wisdom, Good Judgment

Detail of a 12th-century mosaic of Solomon in Saint Mark's Basilica, Venice, Italy

Solomon, the son of King David and Queen Bathsheba, was born in the early part of the 10th century B.C. King David had united the 12 tribes and made Jerusalem the capital of the Kingdom of Israel. Solomon inherited a peaceful and wealthy kingdom that extended from the Euphrates River in the north to Egypt in the south.

Once on the throne, Solomon expanded the kingdom further through military conquests and alliances with neighboring lands. With help from the Phoenicians, Solomon established a large trading empire. An alliance with the Queen of Sheba, whose kingdom lay along the Red Sea route to the Indian Ocean, extended Israel's trading network and brought luxurious goods, such as gold, into the kingdom.

As a leader, Solomon was known for his wisdom. Rulers from other lands consulted him on various issues and his subjects relied on his judgment to solve disputes. One story tells of two women claiming to be the mother of the same baby. Solomon determined that the solution

was to divide the baby in half. The first woman agreed with this solution, because neither woman would have the baby. But the second woman insisted that the baby be given to the first woman, so that the baby could live. Her reaction told Solomon who the real mother was.

Solomon was also known for his extensive building projects. Solomon's temple in Jerusalem took seven years to build, was made of stone and cedar, and included gold overlays. The temple complex included a city wall and a great palace situated next to the temple.

Solomon's building projects strained the kingdom's finances. As a result, high taxes were levied, particularly on people in the northern part of the kingdom. Male citizens were required to work one out of every three months on the building projects. High taxes and forced labor caused discontent and conflict between the northern and southern parts of the kingdom. During the rule of Solomon's son, the kingdom of Israel split in two: Israel in the north and Judah in the south.

REVIEW & ASSESS

1. **Analyze Cause and Effect** What caused Solomon to lose the support of his subjects?

2. **Form and Support Opinions** What do you think was Solomon's greatest achievement? Support your opinion with specific details.

2 CHAPTER 5 LESSON 1.4
Writings From the Hebrew Bible

UNIT

NATIONAL GEOGRAPHIC LEARNING

DOCUMENT-BASED QUESTION

Use the questions here to help you analyze the sources and write your paragraph.

DOCUMENT ONE: from the Book of Genesis

1A What does God want Abraham to do?

_____

_____

_____

_____

1B Constructed Response What does God promise Abraham?

_____

_____

_____

_____

DOCUMENT TWO: from the Book of Exodus

2A Pick one of the commandments and restate it in your own words.

_____

_____

_____

_____

2B Constructed Response What do the first four commandments have in common? What do the last six have in common?

_____

_____

_____

_____

SYNTHESIZE & WRITE

What did God promise the Israelites?

Topic Sentence: _____

_____

Your Paragraph: _____

_____

_____

_____

_____

_____

UNIT **2**   CHAPTER 6 SECTION 1
Indus Valley Civilizations

NATIONAL GEOGRAPHIC LEARNING

READING AND NOTE-TAKING

SUMMARIZE MAIN IDEAS AND DETAILS   Take notes to help you summarize the most important facts and details you encounter as you read Section 1. Write the title of the lesson in first and then summarize the main ideas and details for Lessons 1.1 through 1.3.

Lesson Title: _The Geography of Ancient India_

Main Idea: _The geography of India is diverse, and its weather varies throughout the year._

Details: _____

_____

_____

Lesson Title: _____

Main Idea: _____

_____

Details: _____

_____

Lesson Title: _____

Main Idea: _____

_____

Details: _____

_____

| **UNIT 2** | **CHAPTER 6 SECTION 1**
Indus Valley Civilizations |

READING AND NOTE-TAKING

CATEGORIZE RELIGIONS Keep track of the ideas and beliefs of Hinduism and Buddhism as you read Section 1. Read each sentence below and decide which religion it applies to. On the line to the left of the sentence, write in either **H** or **B**.

____ This religion has many gods and goddesses and developed out of Brahmanism.

____ This religion teaches that the Eightfold Path leads to nirvana.

____ The totality of the teachings that have come down from the founder are known as the dharma, or divine law.

____ According to this religion's beliefs, a person's conduct determines the kind of life he or she is reborn into.

____ The founder of this religion was named Siddhartha Gautama.

____ This religion includes practices of yoga that help a person achieve spiritual insight.

____ Followers of this religion observe cultural practices associated with the caste system.

____ This religion's teachings say that material possessions bring suffering.

____ Sacred texts of this religion are found in epic poems.

____ A god in this religion is Shiva, the Destroyer, who is responsible for all kinds of change, as well as death.

UNIT 2 | **CHAPTER 6** SECTION 2
Indian Empires

READING AND NOTE-TAKING

COMPARE AND
CONTRAST EMPIRES

As you read Section 2, use the chart below to keep track of the differences between the Maurya Empire and Gupta Empire.

Maurya Empire	Gupta Empire
Leader: *Chandragupta Maurya*	Leader:
Time Period:	Time Period:
Location:	Location:
Government:	Government:
Known for:	Known for:
Religion:	Religion:

UNIT 2

CHAPTER 6 SECTION 2
Indian Empires

NATIONAL GEOGRAPHIC LEARNING

READING AND NOTE-TAKING

SUMMARIZE INFORMATION Summarize ancient India's legacy as you read Lessons 2.2 and 2.3. Complete the Idea Web with notes about the inventions and innovations that emerged in ancient India. Add extra spokes and circles as needed.

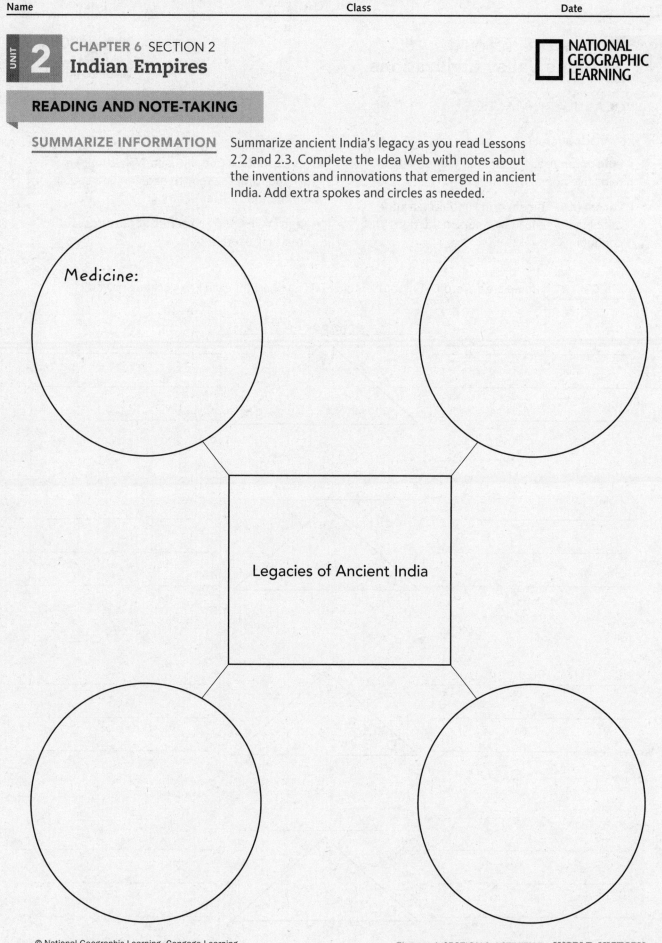

Medicine:

Legacies of Ancient India

**NATIONAL
GEOGRAPHIC
LEARNING**

VOCABULARY PRACTICE

KEY VOCABULARY

- **epic poem** *n.* a long story in the form of a narrative poem

- **karma** (KAHR-mah) *n.* in Hinduism, a state of being influenced by a person's actions and conduct

- **reincarnation** (ree-ihn-kahr-NAY-shuhn) *n.* in Hinduism, the rebirth of a person's soul in another body after death

- **yoga** (YOH-guh) *n.* a series of postures and breathing exercises

WDS CHART   Complete a Word-Definition-Sentence (WDS) Chart for each Key Vocabulary word.

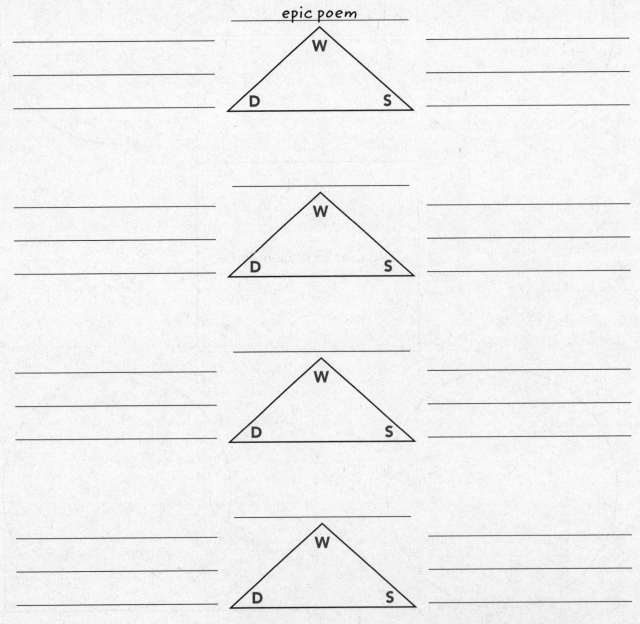

UNIT 2	**CHAPTER 6** SECTION 1

Indus Valley Civilizations

VOCABULARY PRACTICE

KEY VOCABULARY

- **caste system** *n.* a rigid social hierarchy in India that divides people into hereditary classes

- **dharma** (DUHR-muh) *n.* the Buddha's teachings; divine law

- **monsoon** *n.* a strong seasonal wind in South and Southeast Asia

- **nirvana** (nihr-VAH-nuh) *n.* in Buddhism, a state of bliss or the end of suffering caused by the cycle of rebirth

- **planned city** *n.* a city built with a specific layout in mind

- **subcontinent** *n.* a large, distinct landmass that is part of a continent

THREE-COLUMN CHART Complete the chart for each of the six Key Vocabulary words. Write each word's definition, and then provide a definition in your own words.

Word	Definition	In My Own Words
caste system		

Chapter 6 SECTION 1 **ACTIVITY B** WORLD HISTORY

UNIT **2**

CHAPTER 6 SECTION 2
Indian Empires

NATIONAL GEOGRAPHIC LEARNING

VOCABULARY PRACTICE

KEY VOCABULARY

- **golden age** *n.* a period of great cultural achievement
- **inoculation** (ihn-ock-yoo-LAY-shuhn) *n.* a vaccine containing of a mild form of a disease to prevent the development of that disease

DEFINITION CLUES Follow the instructions below for the Key Vocabulary word indicated.

VOCABULARY WORD: *golden age*

1. Write the sentence in which the word appears in the section.

Chandra Gupta II, grandson of Chandra Gupta I, ruled during India's golden age, a period of great cultural achievement.

2. Write the definition using your own words.

_____

_____

_____

_____

3. Use the word in a sentence of your own.

_____

_____

_____

_____

4. What were the greatest achievements during India's golden age?

_____

_____

_____

VOCABULARY WORD: *inoculation*

1. Write the sentence in which the word appears in the section.

_____

_____

_____

2. Write the definition using your own words.

_____

_____

_____

_____

3. Use the word in a sentence of your own.

_____

_____

_____

_____

4. Give an example of how inoculation affected India.

_____

_____

_____

UNIT 2
CHAPTER 6 SECTION 2
Indian Empires

VOCABULARY PRACTICE

KEY VOCABULARY

- **golden age** *n.* a period of great cultural achievement

- **inoculation** (ihn-ock-yoo-LAY-shuhn) *n.* a vaccine containing of a mild form of a disease to prevent the development of that disease

WORD WHEEL   Complete a Word Wheel for each Key Vocabulary word.

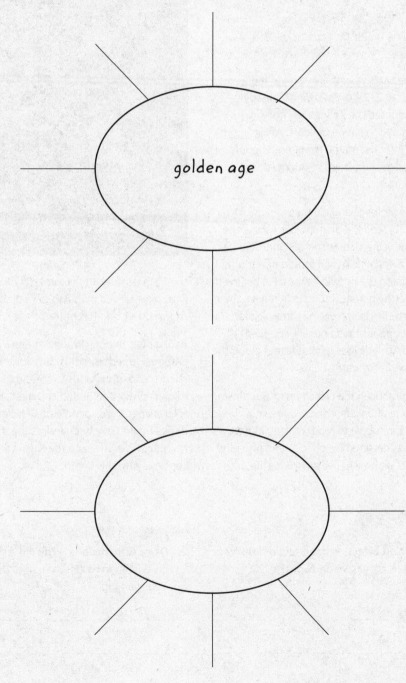

golden age

Emperor Asoka as portrayed on a Tibetan banner

UNIT **2**

BIOGRAPHY

ASOKA

During his reign as emperor of the Maurya, Asoka transformed from a ruthless leader into a devout Buddhist who practiced compasssion, tolerance, and nonviolence to help his people.

- **Job:** Maurya Emperor
- **Virtues:** Compassion, Tolerance
- **Writings:** Edicts on Pillars and Rocks

Asoka, the last of the Maurya emperors, ruled India from around 269 B.C. to 232 B.C. Following a bloody war in which he conquered the Kalinga territory in eastern India, Asoka had a change of heart. After witnessing the pain inflicted on the conquered people, Asoka rejected violence and turned to Buddhist principles to govern his empire.

In turning away from violence and conquest as the focus of his rule, Asoka embraced the dharma. For Asoka, the dharma involved practicing virtues such as honesty, compassion, and nonviolence. Asoka toured his empire, preaching the dharma to the people he met. He believed his duty was to serve the people and to help relieve their suffering. He ordered officials to do the same. Asoka founded hospitals for people and animals, supplied people with necessary medicines, planted trees along the roadsides, and dug wells for water.

As emperor, Asoka practiced the principles of Buddhism. He had his statements of beliefs, called edicts, inscribed on pillars and rocks for people to read. Written in Asoka's own words, the edicts declared his policies and provided advice to his subjects on how to live a virtuous life. In the 19th century, archaeologists discovered many pillars and rocks carved with Asoka's edicts in India, Nepal, Afghanistan, and Pakistan.

Asoka built Buddhist monasteries throughout the empire. He sent Buddhist missionaries, including his children, to other lands to spread Buddhism. Though Asoka adhered to Buddhist beliefs, he promoted tolerance towards people of all religions in his empire. Asoka might have been India's greatest king. However, his religious work—and the Maurya Empire—did not continue after his death.

REVIEW & ASSESS

1. **Analyze Cause and Effect** What effect did the war on the Kalinga territory have on Asoka?

_____

_____

2. **Draw Conclusions** Why did Asoka inscribe his edicts on rocks and pillars throughout the Maurya Empire?

_____

_____

UNIT 2

BIOGRAPHY

DR. MARTIN LUTHER
KING, JR.

Civil rights activist Dr. Martin Luther King, Jr., was a Baptist minister who believed in peaceful, nonviolent protests to bring an end to racial discrimination.

Dr. Martin Luther King, Jr. (1929–1968)

©Alpha Historica/Alamy Stock Photo

- **Job:** Minister; Social Activist
- **Honors:** *Time* Magazine Man of the Year 1963; Nobel Peace Prize 1964
- **Influences:** Jesus Christ; Mohandas Gandhi

Martin Luther King, Jr., was born on January 15, 1929, in Atlanta, Georgia, to a family deeply rooted in their Baptist faith. He grew up during a time when racial discrimination and inequalities were ever-present in our nation. After many years of questioning his religion, King enrolled in a seminary. Here he met Benjamin E. Mays, a staunch advocate for racial equality, who encouraged him to use Christianity to enact change. King later earned a doctoral degree at Boston University, where he met Coretta Scott, a musician and singer. The couple married in 1953 and had four children.

King became a pastor of the Dexter Avenue Baptist Church in Montgomery, Alabama, and, in 1955, completed his Ph.D. In December of that year, Rosa Parks was told to give up her seat on a bus for a white man. When she refused, Parks was arrested. Backed by other civil rights leaders, Martin Luther King, Jr., led a peaceful 381-day bus boycott in response. The group faced violence and discrimination, but the U.S. Supreme Court eventually ruled that public bus segregation was illegal.

After this victory, the Southern Christian Leadership Conference was formed. A key participant, King

spoke out against racism and worked tirelessly to give African Americans a voice. In 1960, King and his family returned to Atlanta, Georgia. King continued to inspire people around the nation with his eloquent speeches and by using peaceful methods to achieve equality. On August 28, 1963, King gave his famous "I Have a Dream" speech during the March on Washington. One year later, he received the Nobel Peace Prize.

King worked throughout the 1960s to bring awareness to racial injustices. Some people said his approach was passive and ineffective, but hundreds of thousands believed in his message. On April 3, 1968, King gave his last speech. The next day, he was shot and killed by James Earl Ray in Memphis, Tennessee. In 1986, a federal holiday was named to honor the life and legacy of Dr. Martin Luther King, Jr.

REVIEW & ASSESS

1. **Make Connections** In what ways can you support the work of Dr. Martin Luther King, Jr., on his national holiday?

   _____

   _____

2. **Synthesize** How did Gandhi influence Dr. King and his life's work?

   _____

   _____

DOCUMENT-BASED QUESTION

Use the questions here to help you analyze the sources and write your paragraph.

DOCUMENT ONE: from the Bhagavad Gita

1A What would you infer about the significance of a poem that runs 700 verses long?

_____

_____

1B Constructed Response According to Krishna, what is special about a soul?

_____

_____

DOCUMENT TWO: from the *Ramayana*

2A Why might Rama describe life as a river in this verse?

_____

_____

2B Constructed Response What comfort might his brother take from Rama's words?

_____

_____

DOCUMENT THREE: from the Rig Veda

3A In what way might a dead person's family take comfort in this part of the poem?

_____

_____

3B Constructed Response According to the passage, what happens to a person after death?

_____

_____

SYNTHESIZE & WRITE

What do the passages from the Bhagavad Gita, the *Ramayana*, and the Rig Veda suggest about Hinduism's attitude toward life and death?

Topic Sentence: _____

_____

Your Paragraph: _____

_____

_____

CHAPTER 7 SECTION 1
River Dynasties

UNIT **2**

NATIONAL GEOGRAPHIC LEARNING

READING AND NOTE-TAKING

DESCRIBE GEOGRAPHIC INFORMATION As you read Lesson 1.1, use the table below to keep track of East Asia's different geographic features. Be sure to include information from the lesson's text and maps. Then answer the question.

Landforms	Bodies of Water	Cultures
Deserts: The Gobi and Taklimakan form barriers to the north and east.		

Describe In what ways did geography shape ancient Chinese civilization?

_____

UNIT 2

CHAPTER 7 SECTION 1
River Dynasties

READING AND NOTE-TAKING

CATEGORIZE INFORMATION   As you read Lesson 1.2, use the boxes below to take notes on the Shang and Zhou dynasties. Then answer the question.

Shang Dynasty

emerged along the banks of the Huang He around 1600 B.C.

Zhou Dynasty

overthrew the Shang around 1045 B.C.

Summarize   What was the dynastic cycle?

_____

_____

Chapter 7 SECTION 1 **ACTIVITY B**   WORLD HISTORY

UNIT 2

CHAPTER 7 SECTION 2
China's Empires

READING AND NOTE-TAKING

CATEGORIZE INFORMATION   As you read Section 2, use the table below to categorize information about the Qin and Han dynasties. Then answer the questions.

Qin Dynasty	Han Dynasty
Shi Huangdi was the first emperor of China who established the Qin Dynasty, and was a strict but strong ruler.	Liu Bang was a peasant who seized control during a rebellion and established the Han Dynasty.

UNIT
2
CHAPTER 7 SECTION 2
China's Empires *continued*

NATIONAL
GEOGRAPHIC
LEARNING

What was Shi Huangdi's biggest fear? _____

_____

_____

How did he supposedly die? _____

_____

_____

What was the purpose of the Great Wall? _____

_____

_____

Who worked on the Great Wall and other building projects? How did their treatment differ in the two dynasties? _____

_____

_____

What were the greatest accomplishments of Shi Huangdi's reign? _____

_____

_____

Who was the first woman to rule China? How did she take power, in spite of the law against women being emperors? _____

_____

_____

What was the greatest accomplishment of the Han dynasty? _____

_____

_____

READING AND NOTE-TAKING

SEQUENCE EVENTS   Describe the process of cultural diffusion that took place along the Silk Roads using the graphic organizer below.

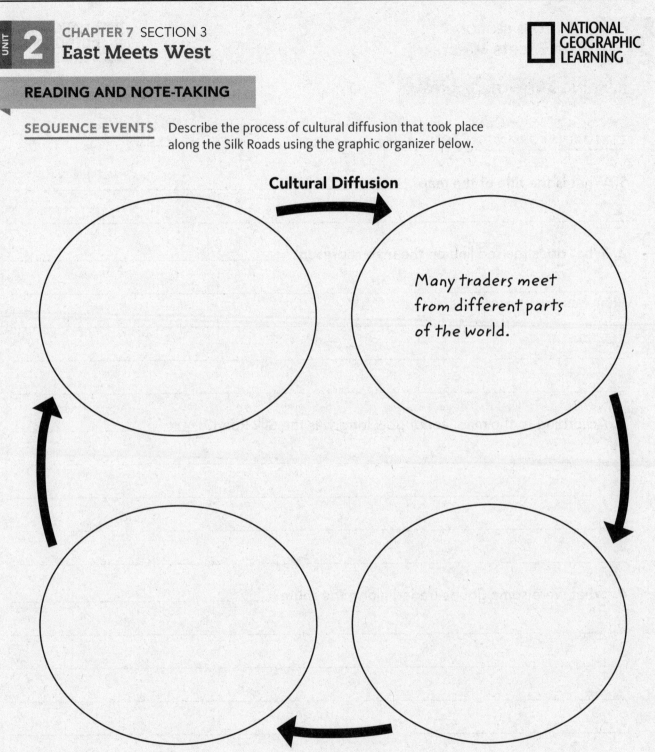

Cultural Diffusion

Many traders meet from different parts of the world.

Summarize   What ideas did the Chinese spread and what ideas did they absorb because of interactions on the Silk Roads?

_____

_____

_____

READING AND NOTE-TAKING

SYNTHESIZE VISUAL AND TEXTUAL INFORMATION   Read Section 3. Then use the text from the section and the text and map in Lesson 3.1 to answer the questions below.

1. What is the title of the map? _____

_____

2. What does the red line on the map represent? _____

_____

_____

_____

3. According to the map, about how long was the Silk Road? _____

_____

_____

_____

_____

4. What were some goods traded along the route? _____

_____

_____

_____

5. How many gold pieces are in the Bactrian Hoard? _____

_____

_____

_____

CHAPTER 7 SECTION 1
River Dynasties

NATIONAL
GEOGRAPHIC
LEARNING

VOCABULARY PRACTICE

KEY VOCABULARY

- **dynastic cycle** *n.* the pattern of the rise and fall of dynasties in ancient and early China

- **dynasty** (DY-nuh-stee) *n.* a series of rulers from the same family

- **filial piety** (FIHL-ee-uhl PYE-uh-tee) *n.* the belief that children owe their parents and ancestors respect

- **isolate** (EYE-soh-layt) *v.* to cut off from the rest of the world

- **oracle bone** (OHR-uh-kuhl) *n.* an animal bone used to consult with the many gods worshipped by the Shang people

I READ, I KNOW, AND SO Complete the graphic organizers below. Write down the sentence in which the Key Vocabulary word appears in Section 1. Then write down what else you read about the word. Finally, draw a conclusion about the word based on what you have learned.

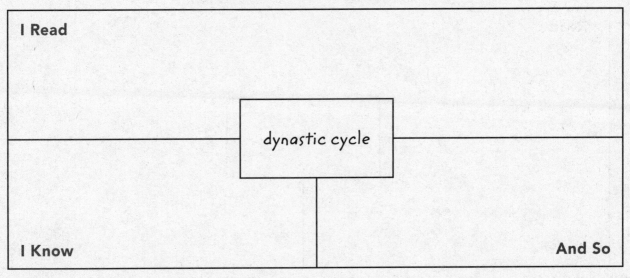

I Read

I Know

dynastic cycle

And So

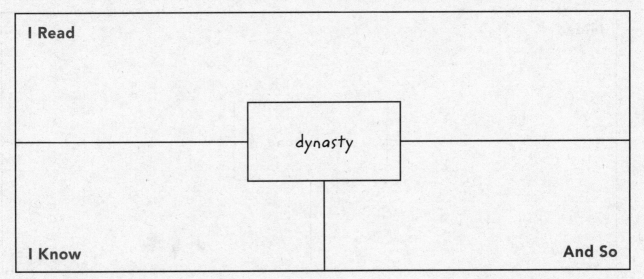

I Read

I Know

dynasty

And So

UNIT **2** **CHAPTER 7** SECTION 1
River Dynasties *continued*

I Read

filial piety

I Know   **And So**

I Read

isolate

I Know   **And So**

I Read

oracle bone

I Know   **And So**

Chapter 7 SECTION 1 **ACTIVITY A** WORLD HISTORY

UNIT **2**

CHAPTER 7 SECTION 2
China's Empires

**NATIONAL
GEOGRAPHIC
LEARNING**

VOCABULARY PRACTICE

KEY VOCABULARY

- **bureaucracy** (byoo-RAH-krah-see) *n.* a system of government in which appointed officials in specialized departments run the various offices

- **emperor** (EHM-puh-ruhr) *n.* the supreme ruler of an empire

- **peasant** (PEH-zuhnt) *n.* a poor farmer

- **silk** (SIHLK) *n.* a textile made from the cocoons of silkworms

- **terra cotta** (TEH-ruh KAH-tuh) *n.* a fire-baked clay

DEFINITION MAP   Complete a Definition Map for each Key Vocabulary word.

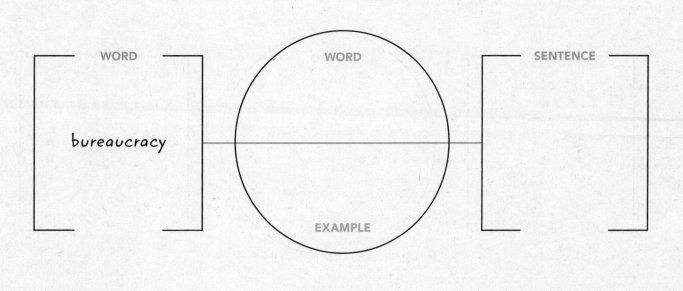

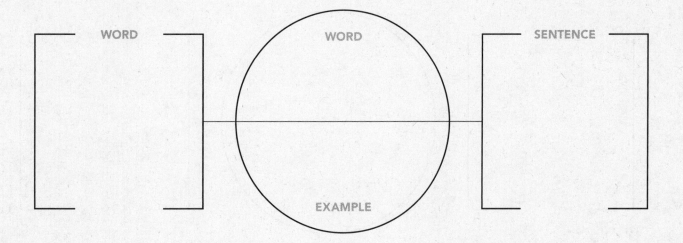

UNIT 2

CHAPTER 7 SECTION 2
China's Empires *continued*

NATIONAL
GEOGRAPHIC
LEARNING

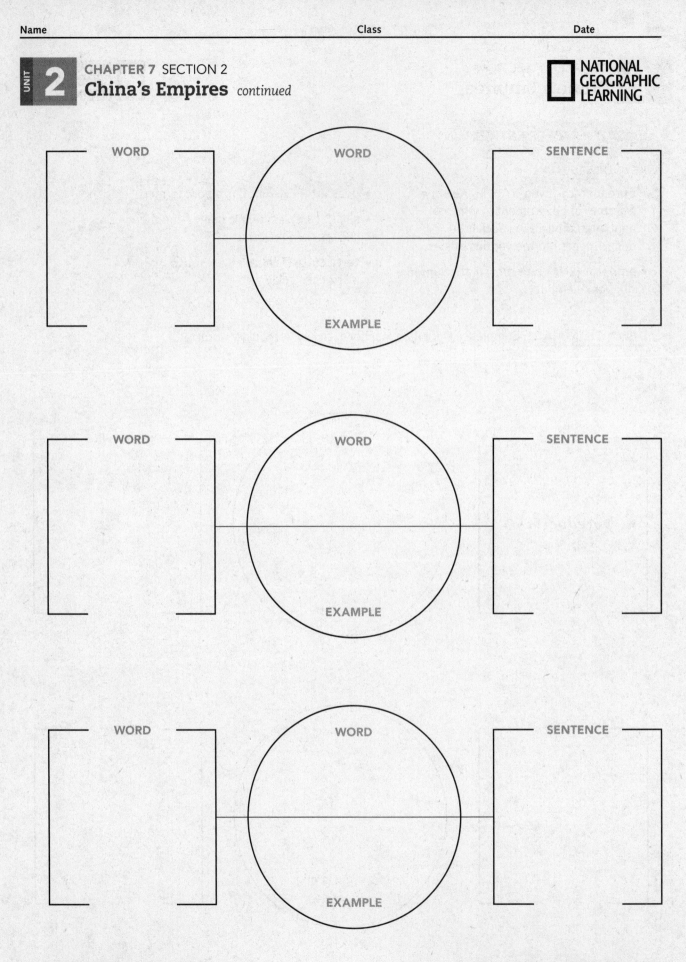

WORD

WORD

SENTENCE

EXAMPLE

WORD

WORD

SENTENCE

EXAMPLE

WORD

WORD

SENTENCE

EXAMPLE

Chapter 7 SECTION 2 **ACTIVITY A**   WORLD HISTORY

UNIT 2
CHAPTER 7 SECTION 3
East Meets West

NATIONAL GEOGRAPHIC LEARNING

VOCABULARY PRACTICE

KEY VOCABULARY

- **barter** (BAHR-tuhr) *v.* to exchange goods
- **caravan** (KAIR-uh-van) *n.* a group of people that travels together
- **cultural diffusion** (dih-FEW-zhun) *n.* the process by which cultures interact and ideas spread from one area to another
- **maritime** (MAIR-ih-time) *adj.* relating to the sea

RELATED IDEA WEB Write one of the Key Vocabulary words inside a circle, along with its definition in your own words. Then draw lines or arrows connecting the circles to show how the words are related, based on what you read in Section 3. Write your explanation of the connection next to the line or arrow.

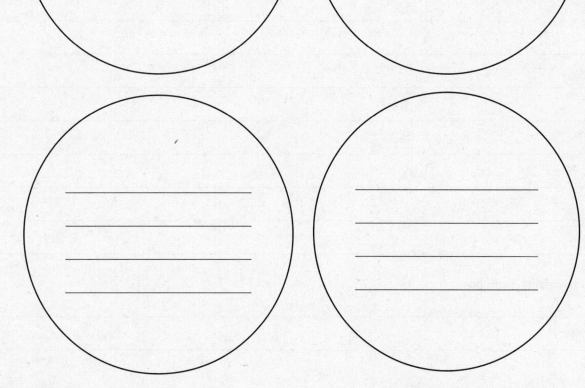

barter: trading goods

UNIT 2

CHAPTER 7 SECTION 3
East Meets West

VOCABULARY PRACTICE

KEY VOCABULARY

- **barter** (BAHR-tuhr) *v.* to exchange goods

- **caravan** (KAIR-uh-van) *n.* a group of people that travels together

- **cultural diffusion** (dih-FEW-zhun) *n.* the process by which cultures interact and ideas spread from one area to another

- **maritime** (MAIR-ih-time) *adj.* relating to the sea

SUMMARY PARAGRAPH Write a paragraph summarizing how the four Key Vocabulary words in Section 3 are related. Be sure to write a clear topic sentence as your first sentence. Then write several sentences with supporting details. Conclude your paragraph with a summarizing sentence.

_____

_____

_____

_____

_____

_____

_____

_____

_____

_____

_____

_____

Summarizing Sentence:

_____

_____

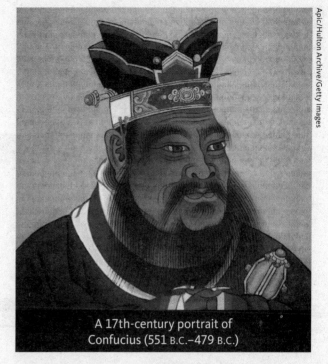

A 17th-century portrait of
Confucius (551 B.C.–479 B.C.)

UNIT 2 BIOGRAPHY
CONFUCIUS

Confucius was a scholar, teacher, and philosopher in ancient China. His ideas have influenced the civilization of East Asia for thousands of years. His teachings formed the basis of a belief system known as Confucianism.

- **Job:** Teacher, Philosopher
- **Goal:** Expand Education for All
- **Quote:** "What you do not want done to yourself, do not do to others."

Confucius was born in 551 B.C. into a poor family in Qufu, China. His father died when he was three years old. His mother was his first teacher. By the time he reached his teen years, Confucius was a determined learner. He was well versed in the six arts he considered important for a good education—ritual, music, archery, chariot-driving, calligraphy, and arithmetic—as well as in history and poetry. His education enabled him to begin a career in teaching when he was in his 30s.

Confucius was the first teacher in ancient China to make education available to many people, not just for aristocrats, as was the custom. He was instrumental in making teaching a profession and a way of life. His purpose for teaching was to improve society by teaching people to live a life of honesty and one based on strong moral principles. Confucius believed that the purpose of an education was not just to acquire knowledge but also to build character. He also believed that people should live their lives by following the "golden rule," saying, "What you do not want done to yourself, do not do to others."

When Confucius was in his 50s, he took on a government job as a minister of justice in the state of Lu. He was loyal to King Lu, but was kept outside his circle of power by other officials. After serving for a few years, Confucius realized that the people he worked for were not interested in his policies, and so he left his position.

Confucius went into voluntary exile for about 12 years. He was surrounded by a circle of students. Eventually, he returned home to teach and to write until his death in 479 B.C. at the age of 73. Ironically, he died believing that he had not made any impact on society.

In fact, Confucius had a great influence on ancient Chinese society and society in East Asia in general. Historians estimate that he had gathered about 3,000 followers. After his death, his followers compiled Confucius's sayings in a collection known as the *Analects*. Confucian ideas spread, and his teachings became required reading for all government officials.

REVIEW & ASSESS

1. **Summarize** What did Confucius believe was the purpose of education?

_____

_____

2. **Make Inferences** Why did Confucius believe that the "golden rule" was a guide that people should follow?

_____

_____

Contrasting Belief Systems

NATIONAL GEOGRAPHIC LEARNING

DOCUMENT-BASED QUESTION

Use the questions here to help you analyze the sources and write your paragraph.

DOCUMENT ONE: from *Analects of Confucius*

1A How did you react to the nature of Confucius' advice?

_____

_____

1B Constructed Response What details in the passage support the idea that Confucius believed rulers had to set a good example for their people?

_____

_____

DOCUMENT TWO: from *Dao de Jing*

2A In your own words, what does this passage suggest people do?

_____

_____

2B Constructed Response According to the passage, how can powerful people live peaceful, happy lives?

_____

_____

DOCUMENT THREE: from *Han Feizi: Basic Writings*

3A What did you think of Han Feizi's approach to governing?

_____

_____

3B Constructed Response What does the passage suggest about the kind of ruler and government Legalism supported?

_____

_____

SYNTHESIZE & WRITE

What ideas about leadership do each of the ancient Chinese philosophies convey?

Topic Sentence: _____

_____

Your Paragraph: _____

_____

_____

_____

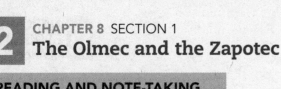

UNIT 2 CHAPTER 8 SECTION 1
The Olmec and the Zapotec

NATIONAL GEOGRAPHIC LEARNING

READING AND NOTE-TAKING

COMPARE AND CONTRAST Complete a Y-Notes Chart to identify similarities and differences between the Olmec and the Zapotec.

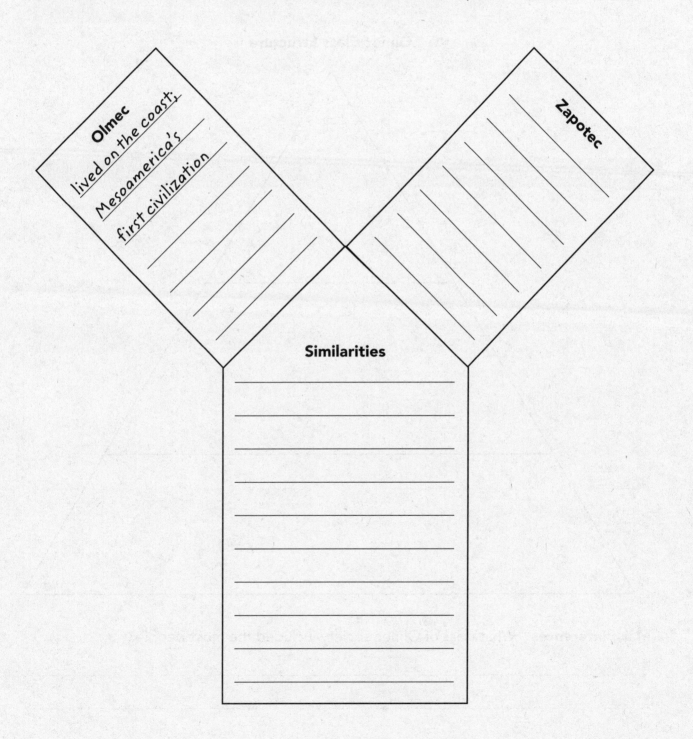

Olmec
lived on the coast;
Mesoamerica's
first civilization

Zapotec

Similarities

UNIT 2

CHAPTER 8 SECTION 1
The Olmec and the Zapotec

**NATIONAL
GEOGRAPHIC
LEARNING**

READING AND NOTE-TAKING

TAKE NOTES ON A TOPIC TRIANGLE   After reading Lesson 1.2, take notes in a Topic Triangle on the class structure of the Olmec. Then answer the question.

Olmec Class Structure

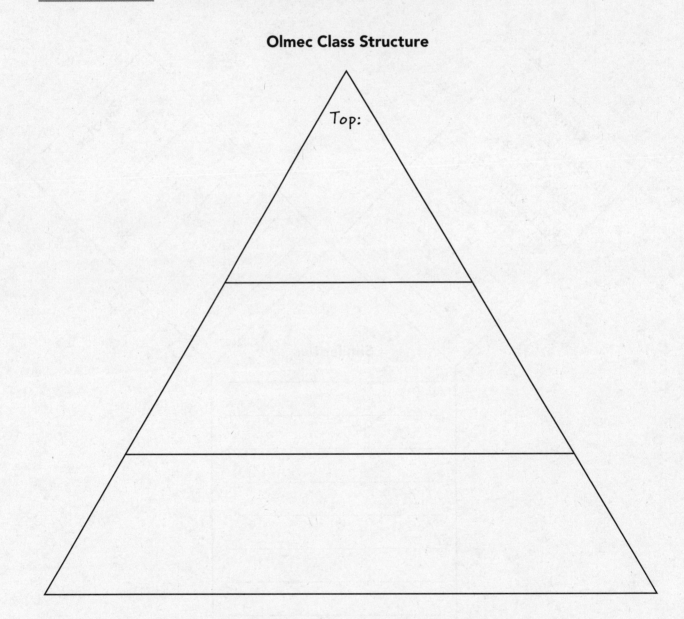

Top:

Make Inferences   What class of Olmec society included the most people?

_____

_____

_____

Chapter 8 SECTION 1 **ACTIVITY B**   WORLD HISTORY

NATIONAL
GEOGRAPHIC
LEARNING

READING AND NOTE-TAKING

SEQUENCE EVENTS As you read Section 2 take notes on a Sequence Chain
to track the development of Maya agriculture.

Maya's Agricultural Success

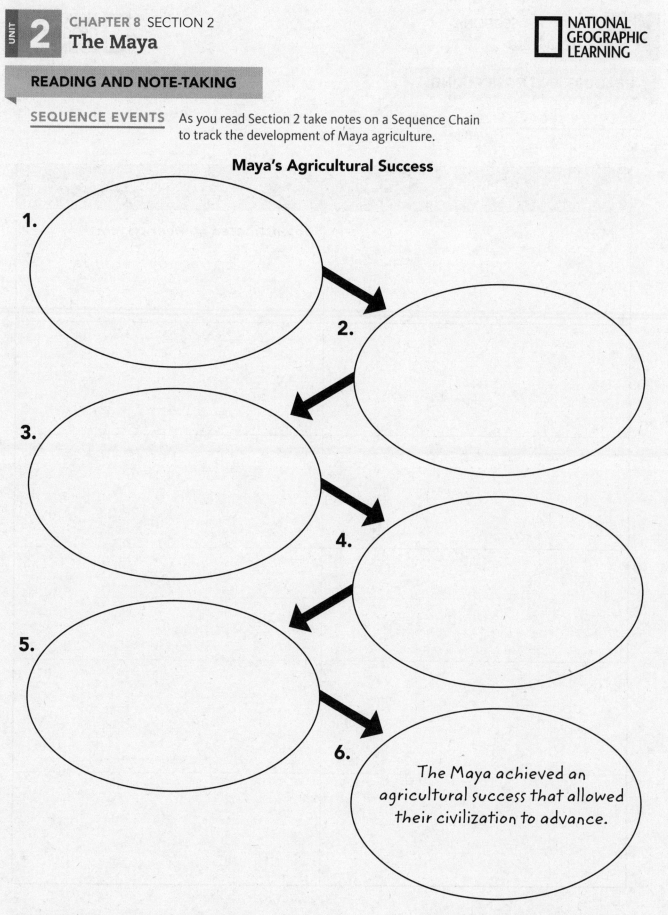

1.

2.

3.

4.

5.

6. The Maya achieved an
agricultural success that allowed
their civilization to advance.

CHAPTER 8 SECTION 2
The Maya

READING AND NOTE-TAKING

IDENTIFY LEGACIES   Use a chart to take notes on the different legacies left behind by the Maya as you read Lesson 2.4.

Subject	Legacy
Math	Sophisticated number system

UNIT 2

CHAPTER 8 SECTION 1
The Olmec and the Zapotec

VOCABULARY PRACTICE

KEY VOCABULARY

- **mother culture** *n.* a civilization that greatly influences other civilizations

- **terrace** (TEHR-uhs) *n.* a stepped platform built into a mountainside

WORD WEB Complete a Word Web for the Key Vocabulary words *mother culture* and *terrace*. Add information, ideas, and related words that help explain the meaning of each word.

Word: *mother culture*

Definition

Word: *terrace*

Definition

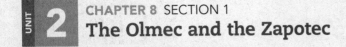

UNIT 2

CHAPTER 8 SECTION 1
The Olmec and the Zapotec

NATIONAL GEOGRAPHIC LEARNING

VOCABULARY PRACTICE

KEY VOCABULARY

- **cacao** (kuh-COW) *n.* a bean used to make chocolate

- **highland** *n.* a type of land that is high above the sea

- **lowland** *n.* a type of land that is low and level

- **maize** (MAYZ) *n.* a type of corn first domesticated by early Mesoamericans

- **slash-and-burn agriculture** *n.* a method of clearing fields for planting

WRITE A SUMMARY Reread Lesson 1.1. Then write a summary of the lesson using all five Key Vocabulary words. Underline the vocabulary words when they appear in your summary. Use the words in a way that defines and explains them.

UNIT 2 — CHAPTER 8 SECTION 2
The Maya

NATIONAL GEOGRAPHIC LEARNING

VOCABULARY PRACTICE

KEY VOCABULARY

- **codex** (KOH-decks) *n.* a folded book made of tree bark paper
- **glyph** (glihf) *n.* a symbolic picture used to represent a word, syllable, or sound

VOCABULARY T-CHART Use a T-Chart to compare the meanings of the Key Vocabulary words *codex* and *glyph*. Write each word's definition and then list details about each word based on what you have read in Section 2. Then answer the question.

Word: codex	Word: glyph
Definition:	Definition:
Details:	Details:

Compare What is one way the meanings of *codex* and *glyph* are related?

_____

_____

_____

CHAPTER 8 SECTION 2
The Maya

VOCABULARY PRACTICE

KEY VOCABULARY

- **creation story** *n.* an account that explains how the world began and how people came to exist

WORD WHEEL   Follow the instructions below to analyze the Key Vocabulary word.

1. Write the word in the center of the wheel.

2. Look in your textbook for examples of descriptions related to the word, or think of any related words you already know.

3. Write your descriptions and related words on the spokes of the wheel. Add more spokes if needed.

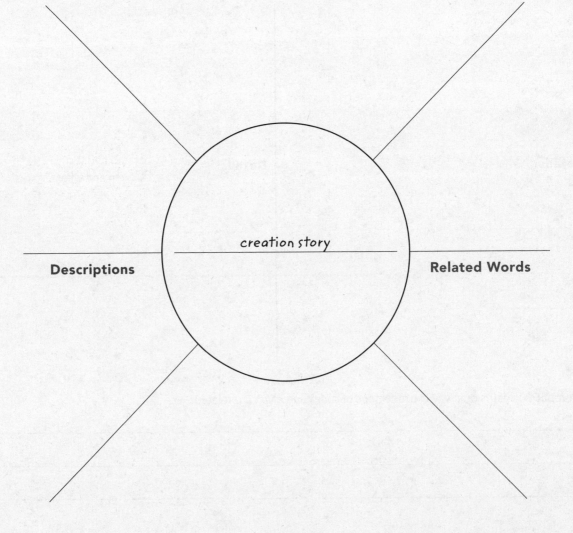

Descriptions   Related Words

creation story

NATIONAL
GEOGRAPHIC
LEARNING

DOCUMENT-BASED QUESTION

Use the questions here to help you analyze the sources and write your paragraph.

DOCUMENT ONE: from the *Popol Vuh*

1A How is this account of Earth's formation similar to or different from what you know of the biblical account?

_____

1B Constructed Response According to this passage, how did the Maya gods form Earth?

_____

DOCUMENT TWO: from the Book of Genesis

2A Restate the information in this passage in your own words.

_____

_____

2B Constructed Response In this excerpt, what was the world like before God brought light to the earth?

_____

_____

DOCUMENT THREE: from *Pan Gu Creates Heaven and Earth*

3A How would you describe Pan Gu?

_____

_____

3B Constructed Response In this myth, what elements formed heaven and what elements formed the earth?

_____

_____

SYNTHESIZE & WRITE

What are some common characteristics of creation stories?

Topic Sentence: _____

_____

Your Paragraph: _____

_____

_____

_____

UNIT 3 CHAPTER 9 SECTION 1
Early Greece

NATIONAL
GEOGRAPHIC
LEARNING

READING AND NOTE-TAKING

IDENTIFY CAUSES AND EFFECTS Use the chart below to record causes and effects that relate to early Greek civilizations as you read Section 1. Write one example of cause and effect for each lesson.

Original Cause	First Effect	Second Effect
The Minoans were expert sailors and ship builders.	The Minoans traded across the Mediterranean.	Trade made the Minoans prosperous and allowed them to build the great palace at Knossos.

UNIT 3 CHAPTER 9 SECTION 1
Early Greece

NATIONAL GEOGRAPHIC LEARNING

READING AND NOTE-TAKING

SYNTHESIZE VISUAL AND TEXTUAL INFORMATION After reading Section 1, study the maps in Lessons 1.2 and 1.5 and use the information on the maps as well as what you have read to answer the questions below.

1. What is the title of the map in Lesson 1.2? _____

_____

2. How many Mycenaean cities appear on the map? _____

_____

3. What is the one other city featured on the map? _____

_____

4. What aspects of Minoan culture did the Mycenaeans adopt? _____

_____

_____

5. What is the title of the map in Lesson 1.5? _____

_____

6. What do the green lines on the map represent? _____

_____

7. What do the green areas on the map represent? _____

_____

8. How are those areas related? _____

_____

9. According to the text, how did the ancient Greeks choose locations for their colonies?

_____

Make Generalizations Why was trade important to the Mycenaeans and the Greeks?

_____

_____

UNIT 3

CHAPTER 9 SECTION 2
Sparta and Athens

NATIONAL GEOGRAPHIC LEARNING

READING AND NOTE-TAKING

ANNOTATE A TIME LINE After you read Section 2, consider the dates listed below. Review the text and identify one event for each year listed. Write a description of the event in the box provided.

594 B.C.

Solon is granted power
in Athens.
_____
_____
_____

546 B.C.
_____
_____
_____
_____
_____

508 B.C.
_____
_____
_____
_____
_____

499 B.C.
_____
_____
_____
_____
_____

Name _____ Class _____ Date _____

UNIT **3** CHAPTER 9 SECTION 2
Sparta and Athens *continued*

NATIONAL
GEOGRAPHIC
LEARNING

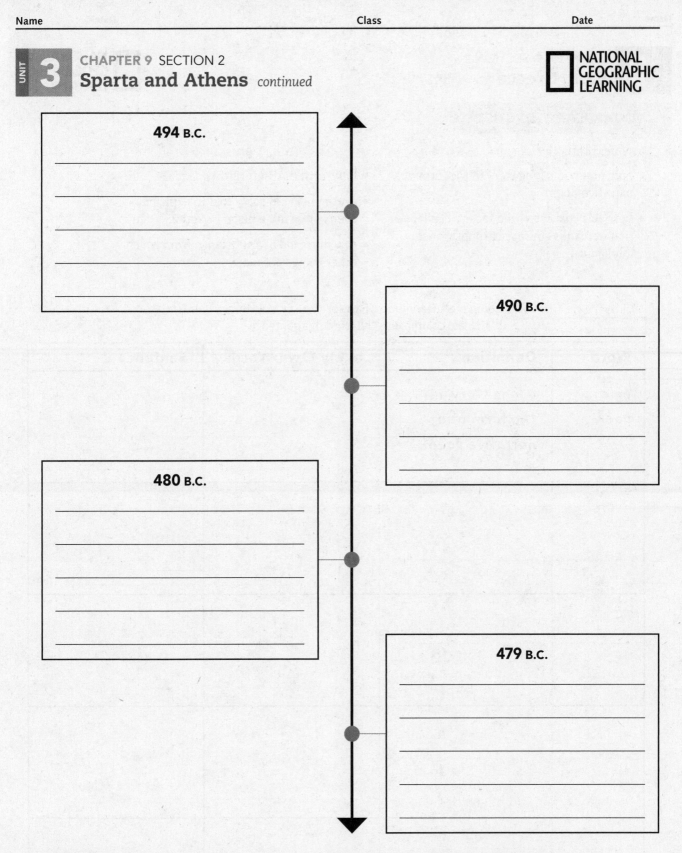

494 B.C.

_____

_____

_____

_____

490 B.C.

_____

_____

_____

_____

480 B.C.

_____

_____

_____

_____

479 B.C.

_____

_____

_____

_____

Identify What factors helped the ancient Greeks to defeat the Persians?

_____

_____

UNIT **3** CHAPTER 9 SECTION 1
Early Greece

NATIONAL GEOGRAPHIC LEARNING

VOCABULARY PRACTICE

KEY VOCABULARY

- **epic poem** *n.* a long story in the form of a narrative poem
- **hero** *n.* a character who faces a challenge that demands courage, strength, and intelligence
- **labyrinth** (LAB-uh-rinth) *n.* a maze
- **myth** *n.* an old story told to explain an event or justify a belief or action
- **raw material** *n.* a substance from which other things are made

DEFINITION CHART Complete a Definition Chart for the Key Vocabulary words. In the last column, use the word in a sentence.

Word	Definition	In My Own Words	Sentence
epic poem	a long story in the form of a narrative poem		

UNIT 3

CHAPTER 9 SECTION 1
Early Greece

NATIONAL
GEOGRAPHIC
LEARNING

VOCABULARY PRACTICE

KEY VOCABULARY

- **acropolis** (uh-KRAH-puh-lihs) *n.* the highest point in an ancient Greek city

- **agora** (uh-GOHR-uh) *n.* an open space in an ancient Greek city that served as a marketplace and social center

- **aristocracy** (air-uh-STOCK- ruh-see) *n.* an upper class that is richer and more powerful than the rest of society

- **monarchy** (MAHN-ahr-kee) *n.* a government ruled by a single person, such as a king

- **oligarchy** (OH-lih-gahr-kee) *n.* a government ruled by a few powerful citizens

- **polis** (POH-lihs) *n.* a Greek city-state

- **tyrant** (TY-ruhnt) *n.* in ancient Greek city-states, a ruler who took power illegally

SUMMARY PARAGRAPH Summarize the development of cities and city-states in early Greece, including the ways governments ruled. Use all of the Key Vocabulary words in your summary.

_____

_____

_____

_____

_____

_____

_____

_____

_____

_____

_____

_____

UNIT 3 **CHAPTER 9 SECTION 2**
Sparta and Athens

VOCABULARY PRACTICE

KEY VOCABULARY

- **alliance** (uh-LY-uhnz) *n.* an agreement between nations to fight each other's enemies; a partnership

- **democracy** (duh-MAH-kruh-see) *n.* a form of government in which citizens have a direct role in governing themselves or elect representatives to lead them

- **helot** (HEH-luht) *n.* a state-owned slave who was part of the lowest class of ancient Greek society

- **trireme** (try-REEM) *n.* an ancient Greek warship

WORD MAPS   Complete Word Maps for each of the four Key Vocabulary words.

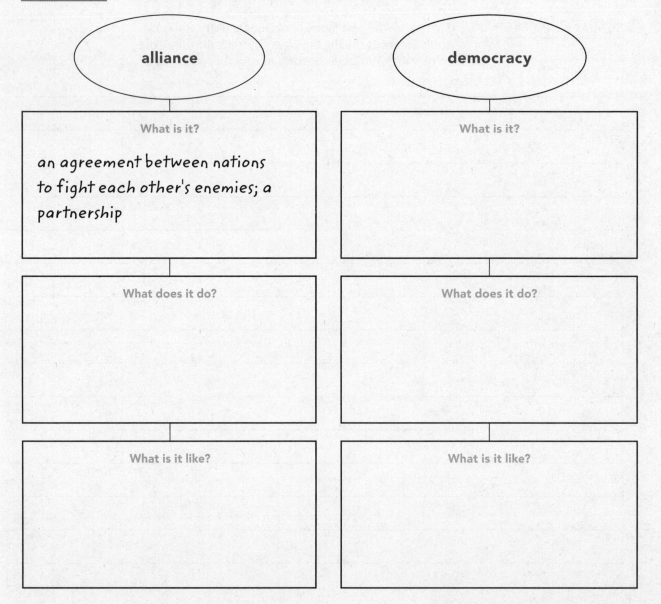

alliance

What is it?

an agreement between nations to fight each other's enemies; a partnership

What does it do?

What is it like?

democracy

What is it?

What does it do?

What is it like?

UNIT 3

NATIONAL GEOGRAPHIC LEARNING

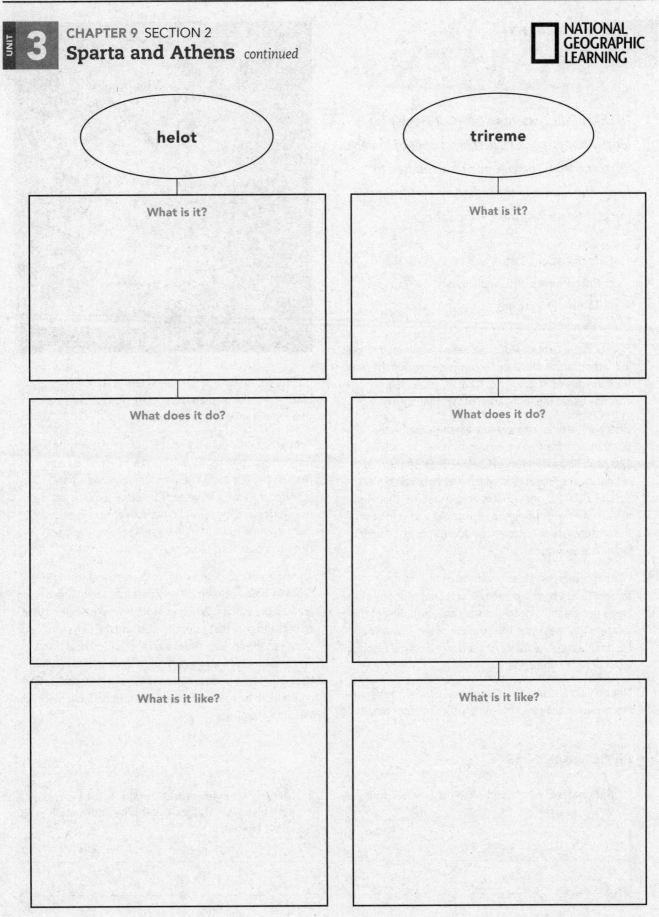

helot

What is it?

What does it do?

What is it like?

trireme

What is it?

What does it do?

What is it like?

Chapter 9 SECTION 2 **ACTIVITY A**   WORLD HISTORY

BIOGRAPHY
HOMER

The life of the ancient Greek poet Homer is largely a mystery. The best clues about Homer's life come from the epic poems attributed to him—the Iliad *and the* Odyssey, *and from the ancient Greek historian, Herodotus.*

- **Job:** Ancient Bard
- **Epic Poems:** *Iliad* and *Odyssey*
- **Talent:** Storytelling

Bust of Homer, the ancient Greek bard

Homer was a Greek bard, or a poet who tells long stories in rhythmic form. Because he composed within the oral tradition, his works were not formally published, but they are considered the foundation of Western literature.

Historians are not entirely sure when Homer lived, but they surmise that he was born sometime between 1200 and 750 B.C. in Chios, Greece. Because the *Iliad* is set during the Trojan War, which may have taken place around 1200 B.C., modern historians theorize that Homer might have lived during the 13th century B.C. However, the ancient Greek historian Herodotus placed Homer's birth date around 850 B.C.

Where Homer lived is also somewhat of a mystery. The ancient Greek bard provided accurate descriptions of the area's geography throughout the *Iliad*—including of the location that was once Troy, the site of the Trojan War. Historians conclude that Homer may have lived along the coast of Asia Minor, possibly in Ionia.

Not only do historians not know exactly when or where Homer lived; they are not entirely sure of other details of

his life, either. One of the characters in the *Odyssey* is a blind storyteller named Demodokos, so scholars believe that Homer may have been blind as well.

Though specific details about his life remain mysteries, the two epic poems attributed to him—the *Iliad* and the *Odyssey*—shaped Western literature. As an oral storyteller, Homer traveled from place to place, telling the stories of Odysseus and his adventures. These stories were eventually written down and became the epic poems people read today.

The *Iliad* and the *Odyssey* differ in style, and so some scholars believe that it is likely that more than one person created the stories. Whether Homer was the sole author or not, all agree that both the *Iliad* and the *Odyssey* provided the ancient Greeks with a cultural tradition, and perhaps even an account of their past, that might have otherwise been lost. Today the *Iliad* and the *Odyssey* continue to be read and studied as foundational pieces of Western literature.

REVIEW & ASSESS

1. **Summarize** Where and when did Homer likely live?

_____

_____

2. **Identify Main Ideas and Details** What sources have historians used to determine information about Homer?

_____

_____

UNIT **3**

CHAPTER 10 SECTION 1
The Golden Age

NATIONAL
GEOGRAPHIC
LEARNING

READING AND NOTE-TAKING

**COMPARE AND
CONTRAST LEADERS**   Use a Venn Diagram to compare and contrast the actions of Cleisthenes and Pericles, two rulers who laid the foundation for democracy in Athens.

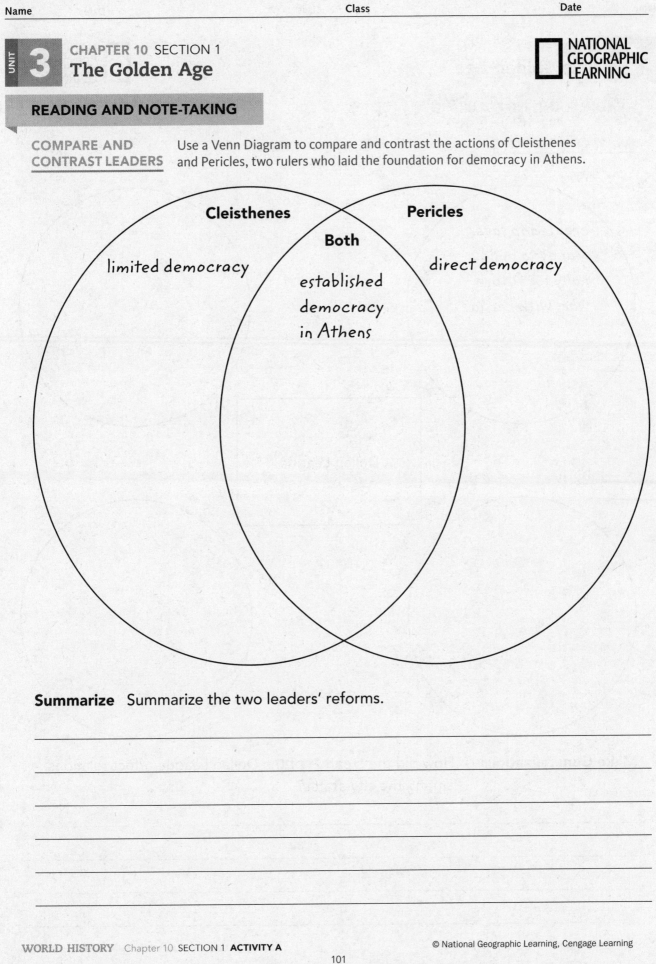

Cleisthenes

Both

Pericles

limited democracy

established
democracy
in Athens

direct democracy

Summarize Summarize the two leaders' reforms.

_____

_____

_____

_____

_____

_____

**NATIONAL
GEOGRAPHIC
LEARNING**

READING AND NOTE-TAKING

DRAW CONCLUSIONS   As you read Section 1, take notes on the Delian League using the Idea Web below.

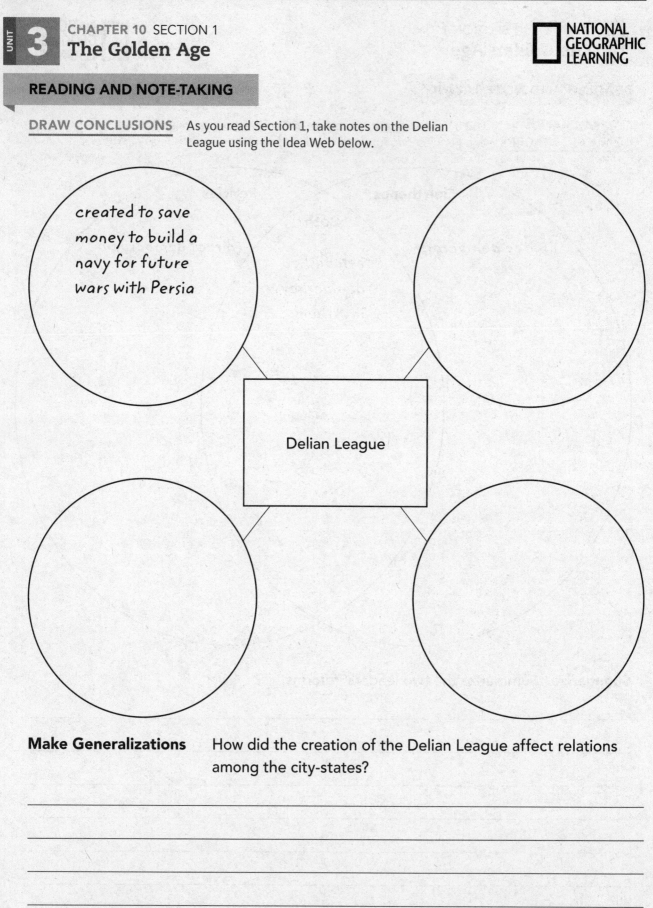

created to save money to build a navy for future wars with Persia

Delian League

Make Generalizations   How did the creation of the Delian League affect relations among the city-states?

_____

_____

_____

_____

UNIT 3

CHAPTER 10 SECTION 2
The Peloponnesian War

NATIONAL GEOGRAPHIC LEARNING

READING AND NOTE-TAKING

SEQUENCE EVENTS AND TAKE NOTES   As you read from Lessons 2.1 and 2.2, take notes on the Peloponnesian War. First write the titles of the lessons and the headers. Then include details from those sections of text. Include between at least four and six details in each box.

2.1 War Breaks Out

TENSIONS RISE

2.1

UNIT 3 CHAPTER 10 SECTION 2

The Peloponnesian War *continued*

NATIONAL GEOGRAPHIC LEARNING

2.2

2.2

Describe How did city-states relate to each other after the Peloponnesian War?

____

____

CHAPTER 10 SECTION 3
Alexander the Great

NATIONAL
GEOGRAPHIC
LEARNING

READING AND NOTE-TAKING

CATEGORIZE ACHIEVEMENTS   Complete the spokes of the Concept Cluster below with Alexander's achievements. Add more spokes as needed.

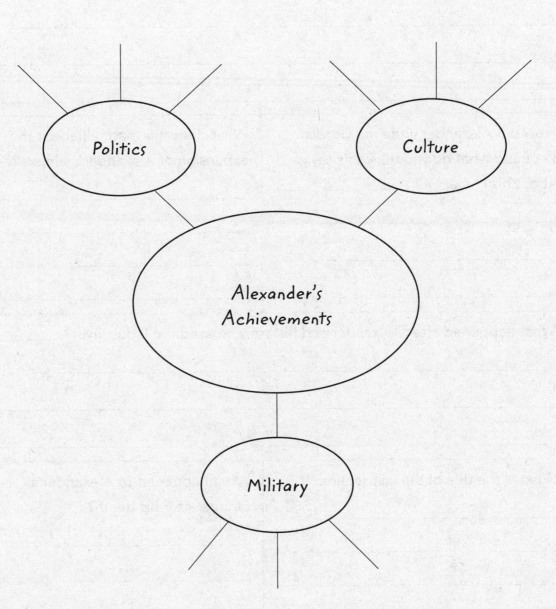

CHAPTER 10 SECTION 3
Alexander the Great

NATIONAL GEOGRAPHIC LEARNING

READING AND NOTE-TAKING

OUTLINE AND TAKE NOTES   Use the Section Map below to outline and take notes about Alexander the Great. Read Lesson 3.2 first, and then complete the Section Map.

What is the title of the lesson? _____

Why was Alexander known as "the Great"? _____

_____

_____

_____

How did Alexander untie the Gordian knot and what do you think this says about his character? _____

_____

_____

_____

What does this map tell about the expansion of Alexander's empire? _____

_____

_____

_____

_____

What happened after Alexander and his army crossed the Indus River? _____

_____

_____

_____

What is the title of the last section? _____

_____

_____

_____

_____

What happened to Alexander's empire after his death? _____

_____

_____

_____

_____

Chapter 10 SECTION 3 **ACTIVITY B** WORLD HISTORY

READING AND NOTE-TAKING

TAKE NOTES ON A KWL CHART Before you read about the legacy of ancient Greece, record in the first column of the chart below the things you know that came from ancient Greece. Then fill in things you want to learn about the legacy of ancient Greece in the second column. After reading, fill in what you learned in the third column.

K What Do I Know	W What Do I Want To Learn?	L What Did I Learn?
Socrates was a famous philosopher.	What did Socrates believe?	He believed in questioning everything deeply, and was put to death because of it.

UNIT **3** CHAPTER 10 SECTION 4
The Greek Legacy

READING AND NOTE-TAKING

<u>COMPARE AND CONTRAST</u>   Using the chart below, compare and contrast the
two forms of drama you read about in Lesson 4.2.

Comedy	Tragedy
humorous	serious

Summary Paragraph   Write a compare and contrast paragraph summarizing the
ancient Greek forms of drama, comedy and tragedy.

_____

_____

_____

_____

_____

_____

_____

_____

_____

_____

Chapter 10 SECTION 4 **ACTIVITY B**   WORLD HISTORY

UNIT 3
CHAPTER 10 SECTION 1
The Golden Age

NATIONAL GEOGRAPHIC LEARNING

VOCABULARY PRACTICE

KEY VOCABULARY

- **direct democracy** *n.* a form of democracy in which citizens gather together to vote on laws and policies

- **golden age** *n.* a period of great cultural achievement

VOCABULARY CLUSTER Complete a Vocabulary Cluster for the Key Vocabulary words *direct democracy* and *golden age*. Write down the definition for each word. Then add information, ideas, examples, and related words to help show what the words mean.

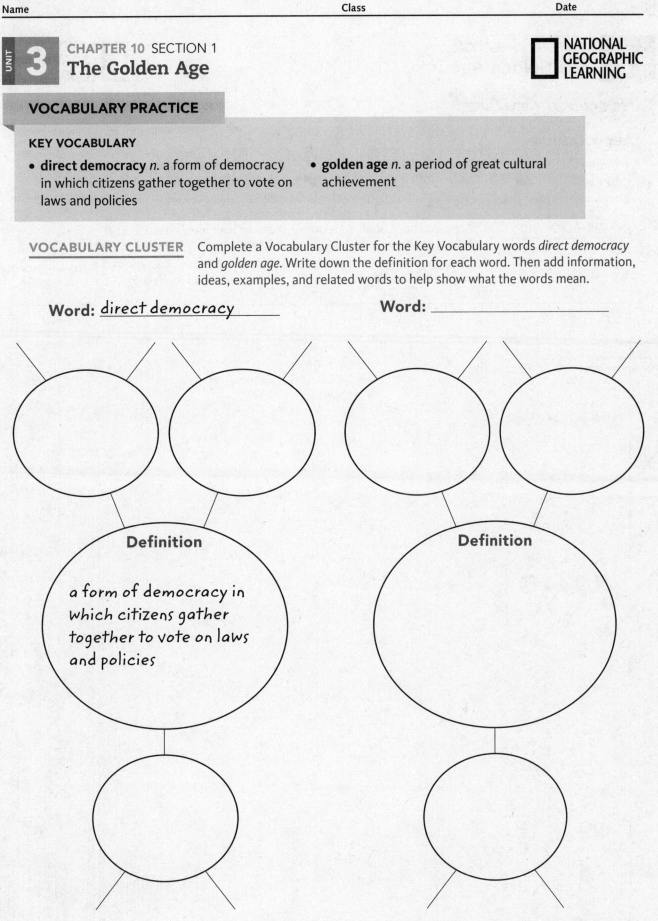

Word: *direct democracy*

Word: _____

Definition

a form of democracy in which citizens gather together to vote on laws and policies

Definition

UNIT **3**

CHAPTER 10 SECTION 1
The Golden Age

NATIONAL GEOGRAPHIC LEARNING

VOCABULARY PRACTICE

KEY VOCABULARY

- **immortal** (ih-MOHR-tuhl) *adj.* able to live forever

- **mythology** (mihth-AHL-oh-gee) *n.* a collection of stories that explains events, beliefs, or actions

COMIC BOOK POSTER   Create a comic book-style poster showing your interpretation of at least one of the 12 Olympians mentioned Lesson 1.3. Write captions or dialogue with speech bubbles to add context to your illustrations. Be sure to use the Key Vocabulary words *immortal* and *mythology*.

Chapter 10 SECTION 1 **ACTIVITY B**   WORLD HISTORY

NATIONAL GEOGRAPHIC LEARNING

VOCABULARY PRACTICE

KEY VOCABULARY
- **plague** (PLAYG) *n.* a disease that causes many deaths

WORD SQUARE   Complete a Word Square for the Key Vocabulary word.

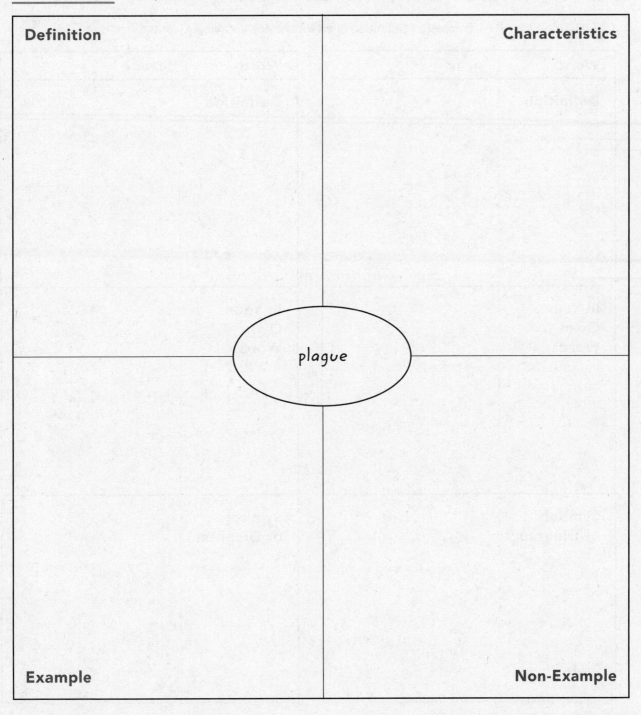

Definition	Characteristics

plague

Example	Non-Example

UNIT 3

CHAPTER 10 SECTION 2
The Peloponnesian War

VOCABULARY PRACTICE

KEY VOCABULARY

- **siege** (SEEGH) *n.* a military tactic in which troops surround a city with soldiers in an attempt to take control of it

- **truce** *n.* an agreement to stop fighting

DEFINITION CHART   Complete a Definition Chart for the Key Vocabulary words.

Word	*siege*
Definition	
In Your Own Words	
Symbol or Diagram	

Word	*truce*
Definition	
In Your Own Words	
Symbol or Diagram	

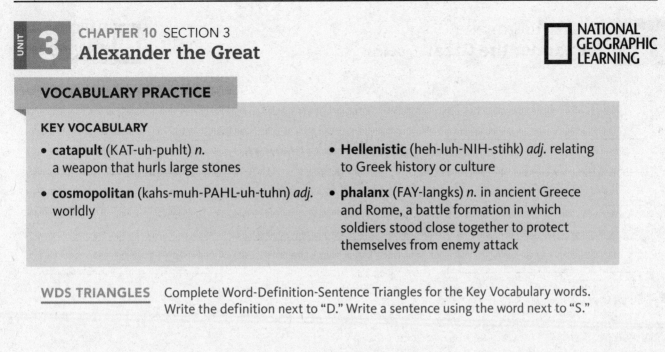

UNIT 3

CHAPTER 10 SECTION 3
Alexander the Great

NATIONAL GEOGRAPHIC LEARNING

VOCABULARY PRACTICE

KEY VOCABULARY

- **catapult** (KAT-uh-puhlt) *n.* a weapon that hurls large stones

- **cosmopolitan** (kahs-muh-PAHL-uh-tuhn) *adj.* worldly

- **Hellenistic** (heh-luh-NIH-stihk) *adj.* relating to Greek history or culture

- **phalanx** (FAY-langks) *n.* in ancient Greece and Rome, a battle formation in which soldiers stood close together to protect themselves from enemy attack

WDS TRIANGLES Complete Word-Definition-Sentence Triangles for the Key Vocabulary words. Write the definition next to "D." Write a sentence using the word next to "S."

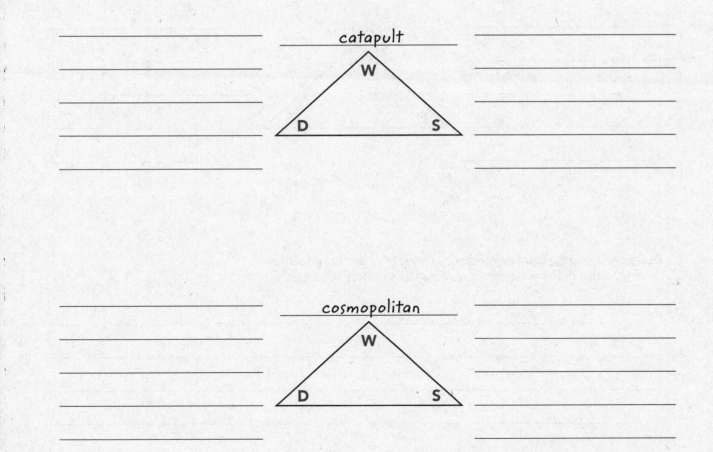

UNIT **3**

CHAPTER 10 SECTION 3
Alexander the Great *continued*

NATIONAL
GEOGRAPHIC
LEARNING

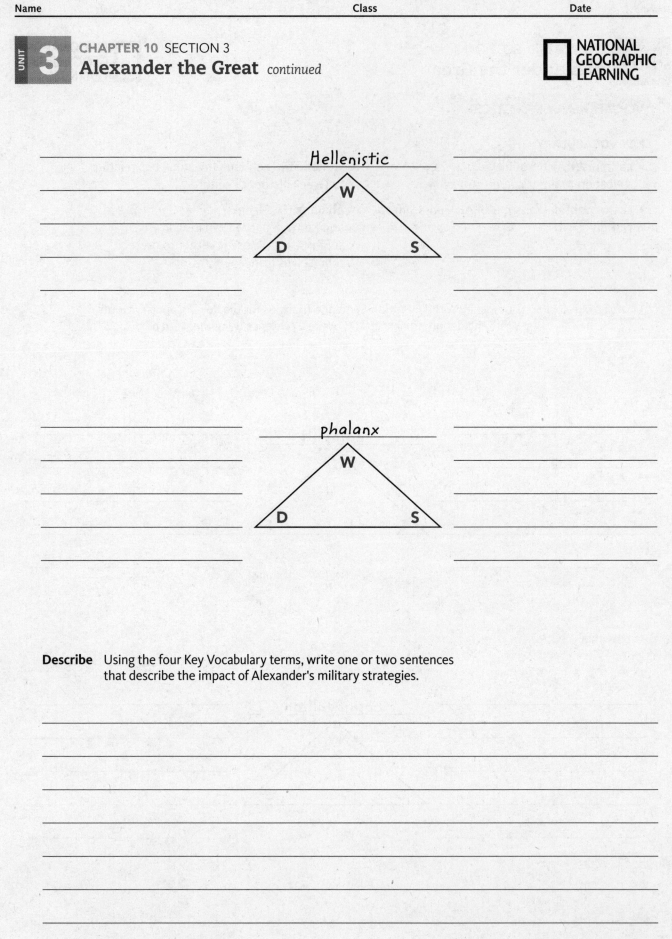

Hellenistic

W

D   S

phalanx

W

D   S

Describe Using the four Key Vocabulary terms, write one or two sentences
that describe the impact of Alexander's military strategies.

_____

_____

_____

_____

_____

_____

3 CHAPTER 10 SECTION 4
The Greek Legacy

NATIONAL GEOGRAPHIC LEARNING

VOCABULARY PRACTICE

KEY VOCABULARY

- **jury** (JOO-ree) *n.* a group of people chosen to make a decision based on evidence presented in a trial

- **philosophy** (fihl-AH-soh-fee) *n.* the study of the universe and our place in it

- **representative democracy** (duh-MAH-krus-see) *n.* a form of democracy in which people are elected to vote on the citizens' behalf

WORDS IN CONTEXT   Follow the instructions below for the Key Vocabulary word indicated.

1. Explain what a *jury* is.

_____

_____

2. Write the definition of *jury* using your own words.

_____

_____

_____

3. Write the sentence in which the word *philosophy* appears in the section.

_____

_____

4. Use the word *philosophy* in a sentence of your own.

_____

_____

_____

5. Write the definition of *representative democracy*.

_____

_____

6. Give an example of a *representative democracy*.

_____

_____

VOCABULARY PRACTICE

KEY VOCABULARY

- **comedy** (KAH-muh-dee) *n.* a humorous form of Greek drama that often mocked famous people

- **tragedy** (TRAH-jihd-ee) *n.* a serious form of Greek drama in which characters endure suffering before an unhappy ending

VENN DIAGRAM   Complete a Venn Diagram to compare and contrast the meanings of the Key Vocabulary words *comedy* and *tragedy*. Then answer the question.

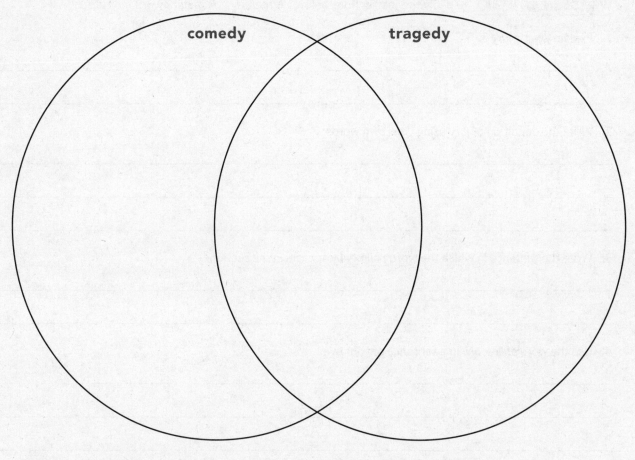

comedy   tragedy

Compare and Contrast   In what ways are comedies and tragedies similar and different?

_____

_____

_____

_____

UNIT **3**

BIOGRAPHY

CLEISTHENES

Cleisthenes is often called the founder of Athenian democracy. He enhanced the reforms of Solon, an earlier Athenian leader. By doing so, he redefined citizenship and expanded democracy in ancient Greece.

- **Job:** Magistrate, Reformer
- **Goal:** Expand Democracy
- **Triumph:** Organized the Council of 500

Bust of Cleisthenes (570 B.C.–508 B.C.)

Ohio Statehouse/Pictures From History/The Image Works

Cleisthenes was born into a prominent Athenian family in 570 B.C. His family was active in the public life of Athens and supported Solon, Athens's leader, in his reform efforts. Solon had made Athenian government more inclusive, but it was not yet a true democracy. Nobles thought that Solon's reforms went too far, while the common people thought they did not go far enough.

Cleisthenes served as chief archon, or magistrate, in the Athenian government between 525 and 524 B.C. He believed that the problem with government in Athens had to do with the way citizens were organized. Cleisthenes argued citizenship should be based on where people lived, not on family lines or wealth. Unless a full reorganization took place, he argued, Athenians would never be rid of hereditary privilege.

After a 20-year period of exile, Cleisthenes allied himself with the popular Assembly to introduce democratic reforms. Athenians had rejected an oligarchy, or a government ruled by a few influential citizens. As leader of the reforms, Cleisthenes organized citizens into 10 local groups. Fifty representatives from each group were chosen randomly to be part of the Council of 500. The Council of 500 proposed laws and debated policies and the assembly voted on them.

Though the government was a democracy, it was a limited one. Only free adult males who owned property were considered citizens. Women and propertyless men had no political rights. However, because of Cleisthenes's reforms, more Athenian citizens became engaged in their government than ever before.

REVIEW & ASSESS

1. **Summarize** What did Cleisthenes believe was a problem with government in Athens?

_____

_____

2. **Draw Conclusions** Why did the reforms of Cleisthenes result in only a limited democracy?

_____

_____

UNIT **3**

BIOGRAPHY

ARISTOTLE

Aristotle was an ancient Greek philosopher and scientist. His theories and ideas formed the basis of Western thought.

- **Job:** Philosopher, Scientist, Teacher
- **Teacher and Mentor:** Plato
- **Most Famous Student:** Alexander the Great

Marble head of Aristotle (384 B.C.–322 B.C.)

Aristotle was born in 384 B.C. in Stagira, a small town in northern Greece near the Macedonian border. His father served as the court physician for the king of Macedonia. When Aristotle was 17 years old, he joined Plato's school, the Academy, where he studied for 20 years.

Over time, differences in thinking caused a breach between Aristotle and Plato. When Plato died, Aristotle left for Assos, a town in Asia Minor, where he connected with a small group of Plato's followers. After a few years, he joined the court of Philip of Macedon. There he tutored Philip's son, Alexander, who would become the famous Macedonian king, Alexander the Great.

Around 335 B.C., Aristotle returned to Athens where he established his own school, called the Lyceum. Because Aristotle walked while he taught, his school was called the Peripatetic school. (The word *peripatetic* means, "to walk about.") Aristotle led the school until 323 B.C. He died the following year.

Aristotle believed that the only way to understand the world was through logic and reason. Further, the search for understanding should be based on observation. His ideas are the basis for the scientific method used today. Aristotle categorized learning into categories, which laid the foundation for the study of biology, law, physics, and

politics. He also devised a method of argument based on the rules of logic.

Aristotle's students continued to teach his philosophy after his death. Later Roman philosophers and scientists also studied his writings. For several hundred years after the fall of Rome, between A.D. 500 and 1100, Aristotle's work was almost completely lost in Europe. Fortunately, Arab scholars studied and preserved his writings. These scholars reintroduced Europeans to Aristotle's teachings during the 1300s and the Renaissance.

REVIEW & ASSESS

1. **Summarize** What were two contributions Aristotle made to modern thinking?

_____

_____

2. **Make Inferences** Why do you think Aristotle might have wanted to start his own school?

_____

_____

UNIT 3

CHAPTER 10 LESSON 2.3
Athenian Democracy

NATIONAL GEOGRAPHIC LEARNING

DOCUMENT-BASED QUESTION

Use the questions here to help you analyze the sources and write your paragraph.

DOCUMENT ONE: from *History of the Peloponnesian War*

1A How does Pericles define Athenian democracy?

_____

_____

_____

1B Constructed Response According to Pericles, what was special about the Athenian system of government?

_____

_____

_____

DOCUMENT TWO: Ostracon, Greece, c. 400s B.C.

2A How effective do you suppose the practice of ostracism was?

_____

_____

_____

_____

2B Constructed Response What does the practice of ostracism tell you about Athenian values?

_____

_____

_____

_____

SYNTHESIZE & WRITE

What was most important in Athenian democracy—the individual or the community?

Topic Sentence: _____

_____

Your Paragraph: _____

_____

_____

_____

_____

UNIT **4** CHAPTER 11 SECTION 1
Early Rome

NATIONAL GEOGRAPHIC LEARNING

READING AND NOTE-TAKING

OUTLINE AND TAKE NOTES   Use the Section Map below to outline and take notes as you read Section 1. Read the section first and then complete the Section Map.

What is the title of the section? _____

_____

_____

_____

Explain the meaning of this section title. _____

_____

_____

How was Rome's geographic location beneficial? _____ _____ _____	Describe what the map in Lesson 1.1 shows. What does this map tell about the geography of Rome? _____ _____ _____
Summarize the legend of the founding of Rome. _____ _____	Who were the early Romans? _____ _____ _____

What is the difference between a patrician and a plebian? Describe their relationship in Roman society. _____

_____

_____

_____

UNIT 4

NATIONAL GEOGRAPHIC LEARNING

Define the word *republic.* _____

_____

_____

_____

What were the Twelve Tables?

_____

_____

_____

Describe the structure of the Roman government. _____

_____

_____

_____

Who was Cicero? _____

_____

_____

_____

How does the painting in Lesson 1.4 relate to the text? _____

_____

_____

What was the Forum? What activities took place there? _____

_____

_____

_____

What are the Key Vocabulary words for this section?

_____ _____

_____ _____

_____ _____

UNIT **4**

CHAPTER 11 SECTION 2
Society and Culture

READING AND NOTE-TAKING

CATEGORIZE INFORMATION Use this Concept Cluster to keep track of information about the lives and rights of different social groups in Roman society. Add more strands to the outside circles to record more details.

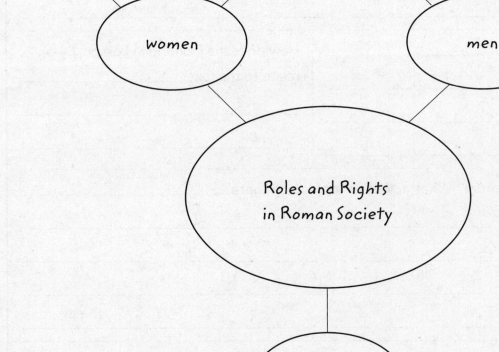

had few rights;
main job was to be a
good wife and mother

women

men

Roles and Rights
in Roman Society

poor people

Society and Culture

NATIONAL GEOGRAPHIC LEARNING

READING AND NOTE-TAKING

IDENTIFY MAIN IDEAS AND DETAILS Use a Main Idea Diagram to keep track of the main ideas and details about Roman religion and beliefs, featured in Lesson 2.3.

Main Idea

Roman religion was based on a pantheon, or a group of many gods.

Detail

The gods had Roman names, displayed human traits and personalities, and controlled particular areas of Roman life.

Detail

Detail

Main Idea

Detail

Detail

Detail

Chapter 11 SECTION 2 **ACTIVITY B** WORLD HISTORY

UNIT 4

CHAPTER 11 SECTION 3
The Army and Expansion

NATIONAL GEOGRAPHIC LEARNING

READING AND NOTE-TAKING

SEQUENCE EVENTS Fill in the Sequence Chart below as you read Section 3 to record information about four important Roman wars. Include when and why events occurred, which groups were involved, and the outcome.

The First Punic War: The First Punic War broke out in 264 B.C. between Carthage and Rome over ownership of the island of Sicily. Carthage's strong navy defeated Rome early on, but Rome responded by building a stronger navy. Rome then defeated Carthage repeatedly and took control of Sicily, Sardinia, and Corsica.

↓

↓

↓

UNIT **4**
CHAPTER 11 SECTION 3
The Army and Expansion

NATIONAL GEOGRAPHIC LEARNING

READING AND NOTE-TAKING

POSE AND ANSWER QUESTIONS   As you read about the Roman legion and the life of a legionary in Lesson 3.1, create your own questions and answers about the topics shown below.

Topic: _Roman legions_ _____

↓

Question: _What is a Roman legion?_ _____

_____

_____

Answer: _____

_____

_____

Topic: _Roman legionaries_ _____

↓

Question: _____

_____

_____

Answer: _____

_____

_____

Topic: _Marius_ _____

↓

Question: _____

_____

_____

Answer: _____

_____

_____

Topic: _Life and training_ _____
of a legionary _____

↓

Question: _____

_____

_____

Answer: _____

_____

_____

Chapter 11 SECTION 3 **ACTIVITY B**   WORLD HISTORY

UNIT 4

CHAPTER 11 SECTION 4
The End of the Republic

READING AND NOTE-TAKING

IDENTIFY CAUSES AND EFFECTS Use the chart below to record causes and effects that relate to the end of the Roman Republic as you read Section 4.

Causes	Effects
The Roman Republic expanded after the Punic Wars.	
	Gaius Gracchus was assassinated.
Sulla marched his army into Rome.	
	The Roman Republic became a monarchy and then an empire.

CHAPTER 11 SECTION 4
The End of the Republic

NATIONAL GEOGRAPHIC LEARNING

READING AND NOTE-TAKING

BUILD A TIME LINE

After reading Section 4, use the time line below to keep track of key events in the decline of the Roman Republic, beginning at 70 B.C.

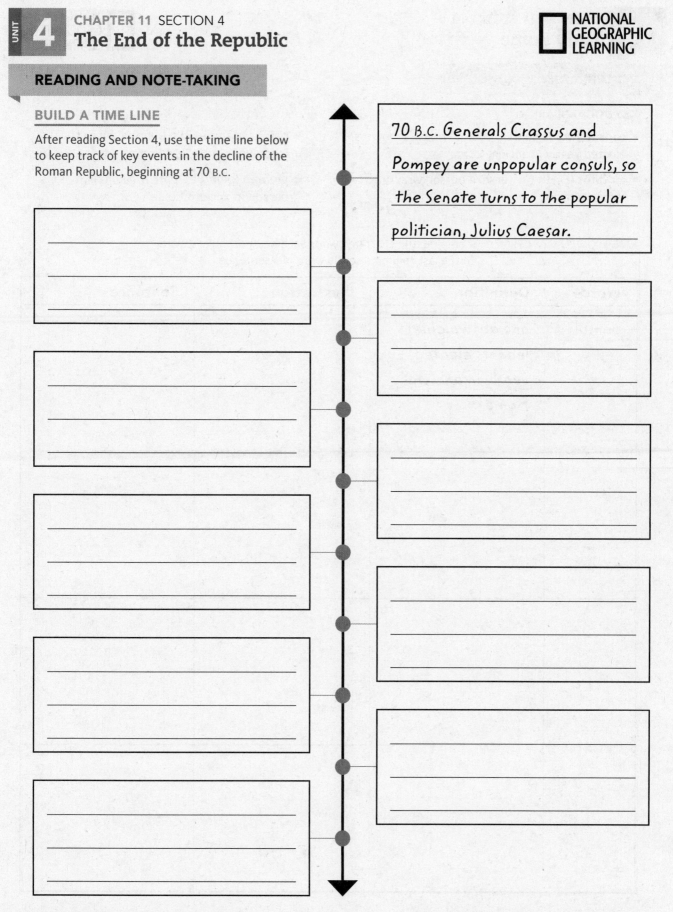

70 B.C. Generals Crassus and Pompey are unpopular consuls, so the Senate turns to the popular politician, Julius Caesar.

UNIT 4   CHAPTER 11 SECTION 1
Early Rome

NATIONAL GEOGRAPHIC LEARNING

VOCABULARY PRACTICE

KEY VOCABULARY

- **consul** (KAHN-suhl) *n.* one of two chief leaders elected yearly in ancient Rome

- **dictator** (DIHK-tayt-ur) *n.* a person who rules with total authority

- **patrician** (puh-TRISH-uhn) *n.* a wealthy landowner in ancient Rome

- **plebian** (pleh-BEE-uhn) *n.* a common person in ancient Rome

FOUR-COLUMN CHART   Complete the chart below for each Key Vocabulary word. In the last column, use the word in a sentence.

Word	Definition	Illustration	Sentence
consul	one of two chief leaders elected yearly in ancient Rome		

UNIT 4

CHAPTER 11 SECTION 1
Early Rome

NATIONAL
GEOGRAPHIC
LEARNING

VOCABULARY PRACTICE

KEY VOCABULARY

- **legend** (LEHJ-uhnd) *n.* a story from the past that is accepted as truth but cannot be proven

- **peninsula** (puh-NIHN-suh-luh) *n.* a piece of land surrounded by water on three sides

- **republic** (rih-PUHB-lihk) *n.* a type of government in which citizens vote for their leaders

- **tribune** (TRIB-yoon) *n.* a representative who fought to protect the rights of ordinary citizens in ancient Rome

- **veto** (VEET-oh) *v.* to reject a decision or proposal made by another government body

KWL CHART   Fill in the KWL Chart for the Key Vocabulary words.

Word	What I Know	What I Want to Know	What I Learned
legend			

Chapter 11 SECTION 1 **ACTIVITY B**   WORLD HISTORY

CHAPTER 11 SECTION 2
Society and Culture

NATIONAL
GEOGRAPHIC
LEARNING

VOCABULARY PRACTICE

KEY VOCABULARY

- **aristocracy** (air-uh-STAHK-ruh-see) *n.* an upper class that is richer and more powerful than the rest of society

- **pantheon** (PAN-thee-ahn) *n.* the gods of a group people, a religion, or a civilization

- **patriarchy** (PAY-tree-ahr-kee) *n.* a society in which men hold all the power

DEFINITION TREE For each Key Vocabulary word in the Definition Tree below, write the definition on the top branch and then use each word in a sentence.

aristocracy

Definition

an upper class that is richer and more powerful than

the rest of society

Sentence

_____

_____

pantheon

Definition

_____

_____

Sentence

_____

_____

patriarchy

Definition

_____

_____

Sentence

_____

_____

UNIT 4

CHAPTER 11 SECTION 2
Society and Culture

NATIONAL GEOGRAPHIC LEARNING

VOCABULARY PRACTICE

KEY VOCABULARY

- **aristocracy** (air-uh-STAHK-ruh-see) *n.* an upper class that is richer and more powerful than the rest of society

- **pantheon** (PAN-thee-ahn) *n.* the gods of a group people, a religion, or a civilization

- **patriarchy** (PAY-tree-ahr-kee) *n.* a society in which men hold all the power

WORDS IN CONTEXT   Write a narrative paragraph about Roman society using each Key Vocabulary word at least once. Use the lower portion of the page to include drawings that might help explain the meanings of the words.

_____

_____

_____

_____

_____

_____

_____

_____

_____

_____

_____

_____

Chapter 11 SECTION 2 **ACTIVITY B**   WORLD HISTORY

UNIT 4

CHAPTER 11 SECTION 3
The Army and Expansion

NATIONAL
GEOGRAPHIC
LEARNING

VOCABULARY PRACTICE

KEY VOCABULARY

- **legionary** (LEE-juh-nehr-ee) *n.* a professional soldier in ancient Rome

- **province** (PRAHV-uhns) *n.* an administrative district of a larger empire or country

I READ, I KNOW, AND SO   Use the graphic organizers below to explore your understanding of *legionary* and *province*. Then complete your own I Read, I Know, and So organizers for two more challenging words from this section.

I Read
A legionary is a Roman soldier who fought in a group called a legion.

I Know

legionary

And So

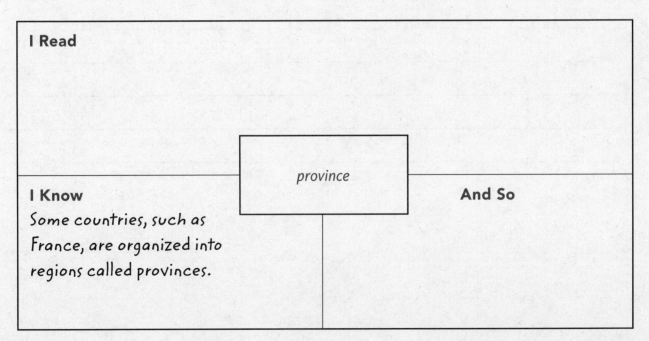

I Read

I Know
Some countries, such as France, are organized into regions called provinces.

province

And So

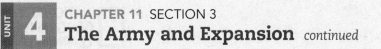

UNIT
4

CHAPTER 11 SECTION 3
The Army and Expansion *continued*

**NATIONAL
GEOGRAPHIC
LEARNING**

I Read

I Know

And So

I Read

I Know

And So

UNIT 4

CHAPTER 11 SECTION 4
The End of the Republic

NATIONAL GEOGRAPHIC LEARNING

VOCABULARY PRACTICE

KEY VOCABULARY

- **civil war** *n.* a war between groups in the same country

- **reform** *n.* a change to make things better

DEFINITION CLUES   Follow the instructions below for the Key Vocabulary word indicated.

VOCABULARY WORD: *civil war*

1. Write the sentence in which the word appears in the section.

He marched his army into Rome, starting a civil war, or war between groups in the same country, and took control of the Senate.

2. Write the definition using your own words.

_____

_____

_____

_____

3. Use the word in a sentence of your own.

_____

_____

_____

_____

4. How did civil war weaken the Roman Republic?

_____

_____

_____

VOCABULARY WORD: *reform*

1. Write the sentence in which the word appears in the section.

_____

_____

_____

_____

2. Write the definition using your own words.

_____

_____

_____

_____

3. Use the word in a sentence of your own.

_____

_____

_____

_____

4. Give an example of a Roman leader who tried to introduce reforms. How successful was this leader?

_____

_____

_____

UNIT **4**

CHAPTER 11 SECTION 4
The End of the Republic

**NATIONAL
GEOGRAPHIC
LEARNING**

VOCABULARY PRACTICE

KEY VOCABULARY

- **civil war** *n.* a war between groups in the same country

- **reform** *n.* a change to make things better

DESCRIPTIVE PARAGRAPH Write a paragraph describing the Roman Republic in crisis using both Key Vocabulary words. Be sure to write a clear topic sentence as your first sentence. Then write four to six sentences with supporting details. Conclude your paragraph with a summarizing sentence.

Topic Sentence:

_____

_____

_____

_____

_____

_____

_____

_____

_____

_____

_____

_____

_____

Summarizing Sentence:

_____

_____

_____

UNIT 4

BIOGRAPHY
CICERO

Cicero was a Roman statesman, orator, and writer in the last years of the Roman Republic. He is best known for his remarkable speeches, particularly for one that foiled a conspiracy against the Roman government.

- **Job:** Lawyer, Consul, Politician
- **Talents:** Speechmaking, Writing
- **Home:** Rome

Marble statue of Cicero (106 B.C.–43 B.C.)

Cicero was born in 106 B.C. to a wealthy family in Arpinium, a town southeast of Rome. He studied law in Rome and philosophy in Greece. Cicero served in the Roman military and was a successful lawyer. Throughout his career, Cicero was involved in several high-stakes political developments in ancient Rome.

In 63 B.C., as consul, Cicero attacked his rival Catiline by exposing Catiline's plan to overthrow the government. After the speech, Catiline and the other conspirators were put to death by order of the Senate. When Cicero announced the deaths in the Senate, fellow senators gave him a standing ovation. However, the Senate had, in fact, overstepped its authority. Roman law forbade the execution of a Roman citizen without a trial. Because of his misuse of power, Cicero was exiled from Rome. After his return from exile in 57 B.C., he never regained the power he once held.

By 63 B.C., the Roman Republic was already falling into chaos. Cicero did not join the alliance with Julius Caesar and the First Triumvirate. He opposed the growing power of the Roman army and urged the government to restore the system of checks and balances. By 53 B.C., the triumvirate had collapsed. Caesar declared himself dictator for life and put forth his own set of reforms. The Senate, however, hated the reforms, and in 44 B.C., a group of senators murdered Caesar.

Cicero was not involved in the conspiracy to murder Julius Caesar and was not present when Caesar was murdered. However, after Caesar's death, Augustus, who was Caesar's relative, joined in an alliance with Mark Antony and another supporter to form the Second Triumvirate. Cicero spoke out against Augustus, and, more vigorously, against Antony. Antony condemned Cicero and in 43 B.C. had him executed.

Cicero's speeches and writings remain among his most important legacies. Many of his writings have survived, mostly in letters to friends. By describing everyday life and events, Cicero's letters provide a glimpse into Roman life during the Republic. The letters also provide context for Cicero's life as not only a statesman but also a collector of art, a country gentleman, and a caring father. In addition to his speeches and letters, Cicero's legacy includes introducing the Romans to the works of Greek philosophers. His translations of their works had a lasting impact on the development of Latin as a language and on the study of philosophy itself.

REVIEW & ASSESS

1. **Analyze Cause and Effect** Why was Cicero exiled in 53 B.C.?

_____

_____

2. **Draw Conclusions** How did Cicero's letters provide a glimpse into life during the Republic?

_____

_____

UNIT 4 BIOGRAPHY
CLEOPATRA VII

The ancient Egyptian pharaoh Cleopatra VII has been celebrated in plays, operas, and films. Many focus on her relationships with two Roman leaders and her supposed beauty and charming personality. However, Cleopatra was a powerful ruler and Egypt's last pharaoh.

- **Job:** Last Egyptian Pharaoh
- **Alliances:** Julius Caesar and Marc Antony
- **Home:** Alexandria

Bas-relief fragment of Cleopatra VII (69 B.C.–30 B.C.)

Bas-relief fragment portraying Cleopatra/De Agostini Picture Library/G. Dagli Orti/Bridgeman Images

Cleopatra was the daughter of King Ptolemy XII, a Macedonian Greek and part of the Ptolemy dynasty that ruled Egypt between 323 and 30 B.C. Born in Egypt in 69 B.C., she ascended the throne when King Ptolemy XII died in 51 B.C. Upon assuming the throne, Cleopatra resolved to restore Egypt's crumbling empire.

Her brother, Ptolemy XIII, who was several years younger, served as her co-ruler because Egyptian custom required a woman to rule alongside a man. Cleopatra sidestepped this custom by placing only *her* name on important documents. In time, Ptolemy XIII revolted against Cleopatra and forced her to flee to Syria. While in exile, Cleopatra plotted to overthrow Ptolemy XIII. She turned to Rome—specifically to Julius Caesar—for help. Ptolemy XIII was defeated and Cleopatra, together with her other brother, Ptolemy XIV, once again ruled Egypt.

In 47 B.C., Cleopatra gave birth to Julius Caesar's son. They visited Caesar in Rome and were there when Caesar was assassinated in 44 B.C. Cleopatra and her son returned to Alexandria. Shortly after, her brother died. Cleopatra now ruled Egypt with her son, Ptolemy XV Caesar.

Cleopatra still hoped to regain some of the eastern territories that Egypt had lost to Rome. To make that happen, she needed Roman assistance once more. She turned to Mark Antony, one of Julius Caesar's generals. Antony welcomed her request for help because he wanted Cleopatra's financial support to conquer an area that included Persia. Antony's plan failed for the most part, but he and Cleopatra were able to return to Alexandria, where he named her queen and her son king. Antony gave Cleopatra the territory in Syria and Lebanon that had previously been under Egyptian control.

In Rome, Antony's rival, Octavian, declared that Antony's actions were illegal and the Senate declared war on Cleopatra. In 31 B.C., at the Battle of Actium, Octavian defeated the forces of Antony and Cleopatra. The pair fled to Egypt where both committed suicide in 30 B.C. Cleopatra's death brought an end to the Ptolemy dynasty. Egypt then became a Roman province, making Cleopatra the last Egyptian pharaoh.

REVIEW & ASSESS

1. **Summarize** What did Cleopatra do to try to regain territories that Egypt had lost to Rome?

_____

_____

2. **Form and Support Opinions** Do you think Cleopatra was a strong ruler? Give reasons for your opinion.

_____

_____

© National Geographic Learning, Cengage Learning

The Assassination of Julius Caesar

NATIONAL GEOGRAPHIC LEARNING

DOCUMENT-BASED QUESTION

Use the questions here to help you analyze the sources and write your paragraph.

DOCUMENT ONE: from Silver Denarius of Marcus Junius Brutus, Macedonia, 43–42 B.C.

1A How would you describe the coin?

_____

_____

1B Constructed Response What did Roman leaders want people to remember about Caesar when they saw the commemorative coin?

_____

DOCUMENT TWO: from *The Lives of the Twelve Caesars*

2A Why do you suppose so many people participated in Caesar's assassination?

_____

_____

2B Constructed Response What does the violence of Caesar's death tell about the liberators' view of Caesar?

_____

DOCUMENT THREE: from William Shakespeare's *Julius Caesar*

3A Do you agree that "the evil that men do lives after them"?

_____

_____

3B Constructed Response According to Mark Antony, why was Caesar assassinated?

_____

SYNTHESIZE & WRITE

What do the Roman leaders' actions and words tell about their view of Caesar?

Topic Sentence: _____

_____

Your Paragraph: _____

_____

_____

READING AND NOTE-TAKING

IDENTIFY PROBLEMS AND SOLUTIONS   As you read Section 1, complete a chart to identify problems different leaders and groups faced and solved during the Roman Empire.

Problem	Solution
Octavian found himself in a deadly power struggle after the death of Caesar.	He killed Caesar's assassins, defeated his rivals, and crushed revolts.

READING AND NOTE-TAKING

SYNTHESIZE VISUAL AND TEXTUAL INFORMATION Use visual and textual information from Section 1 to answer the questions below.

What kinds of products did Rome trade with Egypt? _____

_____

_____

Where did the trade routes go in the east? _____

_____

_____

What was an arch and why was it used? _____

_____

_____

Why might the Colosseum have been built with bowl-shaped sides? _____

_____

_____

What is a mosaic made of? _____

_____

What art did the Romans learn from the ancient Greeks? _____

_____

What is the substance covering the man's body in the photograph in Lesson 1.6?

_____

What volcano was responsible for the devastation at Pompeii?

_____

_____

READING AND NOTE-TAKING

IDENTIFY HISTORICAL FIGURES After you read Section 2, use the descriptions below to identify historical figures involved in early Christianity. Write the name of the person that matches each description. You may use the names of some figures more than once.

Christianity is centered on his teachings. _____

He blamed the great fire of Rome on the Christians. _____

He was the first Roman emperor who converted to Christianity. _____

He wrote epistles explaining Jesus' teachings. _____

He included the Parable of the Good Samaritan in his gospel. _____

He was born into a poor family around 6 B.C. _____

He sentenced Jesus to die by crucifixion. _____

He was killed in a Roman massacre of Christians in A.D. 64. _____

He made Christianity the official religion of Rome. _____

He used parables to teach. _____

They were Jesus' closest followers who helped spread his teachings. _____

READING AND NOTE-TAKING

INTERPRET MAPS   After you read Section 2, review the map in Lesson 2.2 and use it to answer the questions below.

What is the title of the map? _____

_____

What do the orange areas on the map represent? _____

_____

What do the yellow areas on the map represent? _____

_____

What do the largest orange areas have in common? _____

_____

_____

About how long did it take for Christianity to spread through the empire? _____

_____

_____

How would you describe the expansion of Christianity during this time? _____

_____

_____

What area to the east of the empire was largely untouched by Christianity? _____

_____

_____

What generalizations can you make about the spread of Christianity in the Roman Empire?

_____

_____

UNIT 4

CHAPTER 12 SECTION 3
Decline and Fall

READING AND NOTE-TAKING

MAKE GENERALIZATIONS After you finish reading about the fall of the Roman Empire in Section 3, read these excerpts from the text. Then, using your own words, write one or two generalizations about each excerpt.

1. **Excerpt:** "At its height, the Roman Empire stretched from Scotland to the Sahara, an area about half the size of the United States. This vast expanse, with huge geographic and cultural differences, was very difficult to govern effectively. Defending such a large area also proved difficult."

   Generalization: Large geographic areas are difficult to govern and to defend against invaders.

2. **Excerpt:** "Constant warfare also ruined the economy. Trade was interrupted, and the empire had to rely on its inadequate agricultural resources. The people suffered food shortages and higher taxes."

   Generalization:

3. **Excerpt:** "Diocletian had a radical plan: In A.D. 285, he divided the empire in two. Diocletian ruled the Eastern Roman Empire, and his trusted friend Maximian ruled the Western Roman Empire. Each man appointed a junior emperor to rule with him."

Generalization:

4. **Excerpt:** "Diocletian and Constantine only delayed the end of the Western Roman Empire. The end came in the form of barbarians, a Greek word Romans used to describe all people outside of the empire."

Generalization:

CHAPTER 12 SECTION 4
The Legacy of Rome

NATIONAL
GEOGRAPHIC
LEARNING

READING AND NOTE-TAKING

ORGANIZE INFORMATION   Use the table below to organize information about
the legacy of Rome after you read Section 4.

Category	Legacy	Examples
Language	Latin became very influential, it became the source of other languages, and English borrowed words from it.	French the word campus prefixes and suffixes in English
Literature		
Philosophy		
Art		

Category	Legacy	Examples
Architecture		
Law and Government		
Engineering		

UNIT 4

CHAPTER 12 SECTION 1
Life During the Empire

NATIONAL GEOGRAPHIC LEARNING

VOCABULARY PRACTICE

KEY VOCABULARY

- **aqueduct** (AK-wih-duhkt) *n.* a long stone channel that carries clean water

- **arch** *n.* a curved structure over an opening

- **gladiator** (GLA-dee-ay-tuhr) *n.* a man in ancient Rome who fought others for entertainment

RELATED IDEA WEB Write one of the Key Vocabulary words inside a circle, along with its definition in your own words. Then draw lines or arrows connecting the circles to show how the words are related, based on what you read in Section 1. Write your explanation of the connection next to the line or arrow.

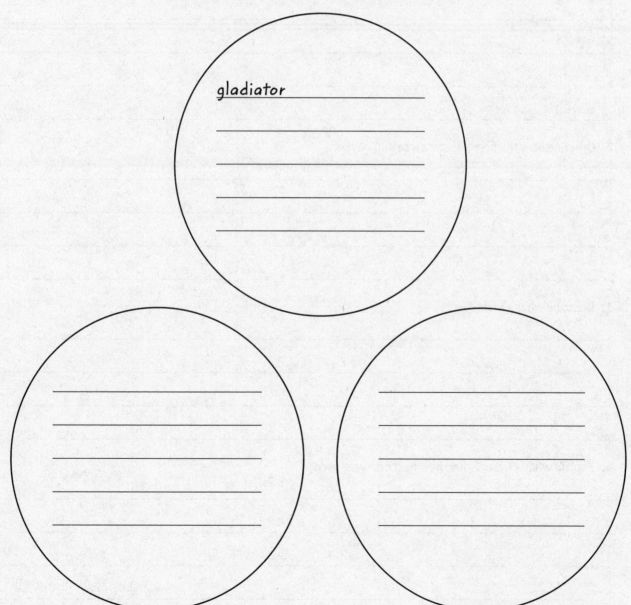

gladiator _____

UNIT 4

CHAPTER 12 SECTION 1
Life During the Empire

NATIONAL GEOGRAPHIC LEARNING

VOCABULARY PRACTICE

KEY VOCABULARY

- **emperor** (EHM-puh-ruhr) *n.* the supreme ruler of an empire
- **fresco** (FREHS-koh) *n.* a picture painted directly onto a wall
- **mosaic** (moh-ZAY-ick) *n.* a grouping of tiny colored stone cubes set in mortar to create a picture or design

WORDS IN CONTEXT   Follow the directions for using the Key Vocabulary words in context.

1. Explain what an *emperor* was.

_____

_____

_____

_____

2. Describe how the first *emperor* came into power.

_____

_____

_____

_____

3. Describe what a *mosaic* is.

_____

_____

_____

_____

4. Explain what a *fresco* is, and how frescoes were used.

_____

_____

_____

_____

UNIT 4

CHAPTER 12 SECTION 2
Christianity

NATIONAL GEOGRAPHIC LEARNING

VOCABULARY PRACTICE

KEY VOCABULARY

- **catacomb** (KA-tuh-kohm) *n.* a hidden underground chamber where people are buried

- **epistle** (ih-PIH-suhl) *n.* a letter

- **missionary** (MIH-shuh-nair-ee) *n.* a person who goes to another country to do religious work; a person who tries to spread Christianity to others

- **parable** (PAIR-uh-buhl) *n.* in the Bible, a short story about everyday life

- **pope** *n.* the leader of the Roman Catholic Church

WORD SQUARE Complete a Word Square for the Key Vocabulary words.

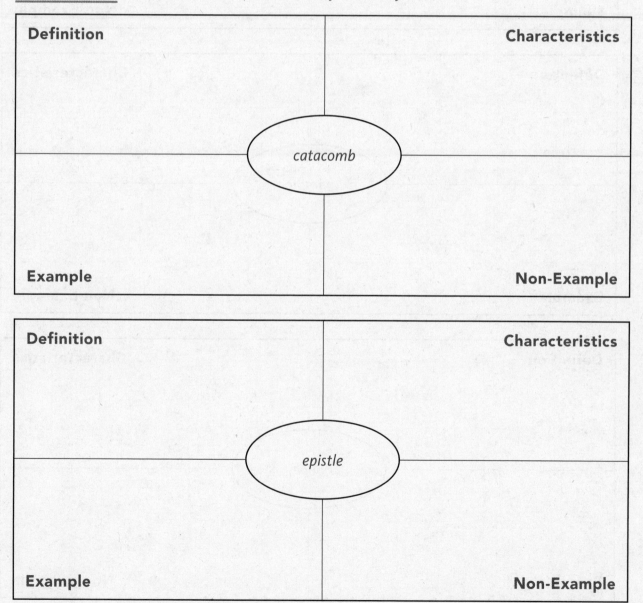

UNIT **4** **CHAPTER 12** SECTION 2
Christianity *continued*

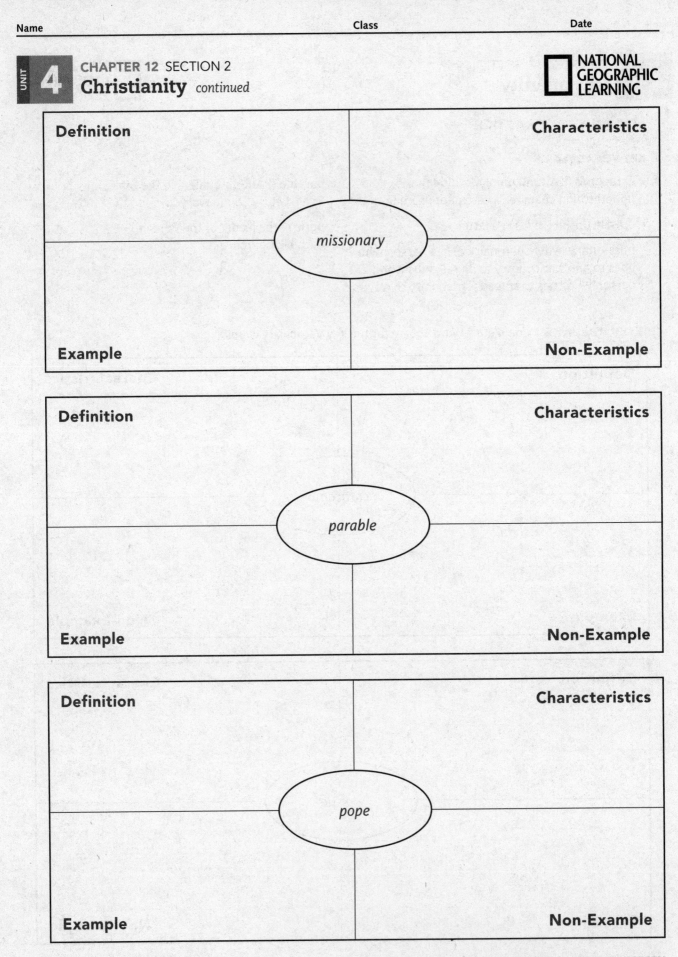

Definition | Characteristics

missionary

Example | Non-Example

Definition | Characteristics

parable

Example | Non-Example

Definition | Characteristics

pope

Example | Non-Example

UNIT 4
CHAPTER 12 SECTION 3
Decline and Fall

NATIONAL
GEOGRAPHIC
LEARNING

VOCABULARY PRACTICE

KEY VOCABULARY

- **barbarian** (bahr-BAIR-ee-uhn) *n.* in this context, a person who lived outside the Roman Empire

WORD MAP Complete a Word Map for the Key Vocabulary word.

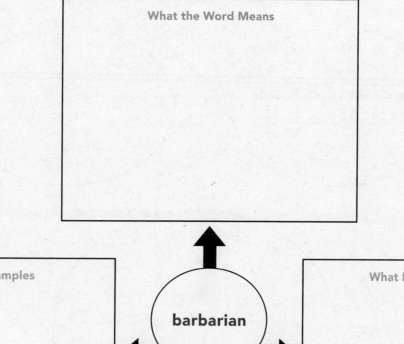

What the Word Means

Examples

barbarian

What It Is Like

Summarize Write a sentence explaining who the barbarians were and what effect they had on the Roman Empire.

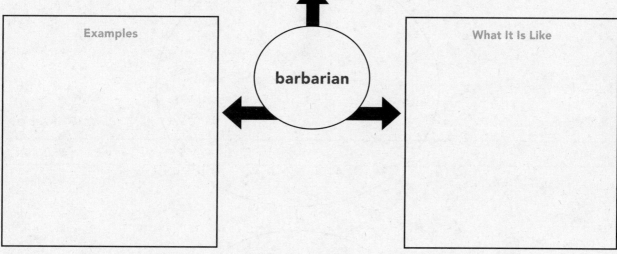

_____

_____

_____

_____

UNIT 4

CHAPTER 12 SECTION 3
Decline and Fall

NATIONAL GEOGRAPHIC LEARNING

VOCABULARY PRACTICE

KEY VOCABULARY
- **tetrarchy** (TEH-trahr-kee) *n.* a system of rule by four emperors

VOCABULARY CLUSTER Complete the Vocabulary Cluster below for the Key Vocabulary word *tetrarchy*. Write the definition in the center.

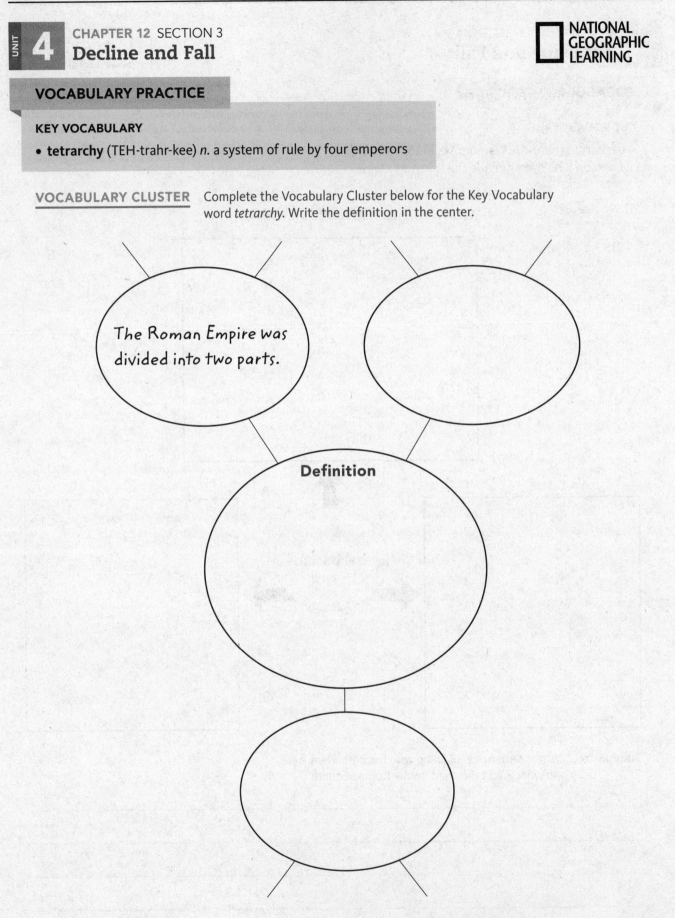

The Roman Empire was divided into two parts.

Definition

UNIT 4 — CHAPTER 12 SECTION 4
The Legacy of Rome

VOCABULARY PRACTICE

KEY VOCABULARY

- **bas-relief** (bah ruh-LEEF) *n.* a realistic sculpture with figures raised against a flat background

- **oratory** (OHR-uh-tohr-ee) *n.* the art of public speaking

WORD MAP   Complete a Word Map for the Key Vocabulary words.

What the Word Means

Examples

bas-relief

What It Is Like

Identify   What are some examples of bas-relief sculpture?

_____ _____

_____ _____

_____ _____

_____ _____

UNIT 4

CHAPTER 12 SECTION 4
The Legacy of Rome *continued*

NATIONAL GEOGRAPHIC LEARNING

What the Word Means

Examples

oratory

What It Is Like

Make Inferences   List examples of occupations for which you need good oratory skills.

_____   _____

_____   _____

_____   _____

_____   _____

UNIT 4 BIOGRAPHY
PAUL

Paul, also known as Saul of Tarsus, is considered one of the most influential early Christian missionaries and church leaders. His letters, which make up several books of the New Testament, helped shaped early Christianity.

- **Job:** Tent Maker, Apostle
- **Notable Moment:** Conversion to Christianity
- **Skill:** Epistle Writing

Paul was born around A.D. 10 in the city of Tarsus, located in present-day Turkey. He was a well-educated Jew and a Roman citizen. According to his writings in the New Testament, Paul was a tent maker by trade.

Paul was brought up to strictly follow the Jewish laws, and he did so with zeal. At first, he was an enemy of early Christianity. He spent much of the first half of his life traveling to synagogues, arresting and persecuting people involved in the growing Christian movement.

According to Paul's own account, he converted to Christianity while on the road to Damascus to visit the synagogues there. He claimed that on his journey, a bright light shone on him and he had a vision in which Jesus revealed himself as the Son of God. The incident changed Paul, and from that time on, he began spreading Jesus' teachings. Paul had never met Jesus, so he sought out Peter, an apostle of Jesus, to learn how Jesus lived.

Paul traveled throughout Asia Minor and Greece, gaining converts and setting up churches. He wrote letters, called epistles, which explained Jesus' teachings. His epistles, originally written in Greek, make up 13 of the

Mosaic of Paul (A.D. 10 – A.D. 64) in Chora Church, Istanbul, Turkey

Hans Lippert/Westend61 RM/Age Fotostock

27 books of the New Testament. The epistles were sent to early churches and individuals and they included explanations of the gospels, solutions to local problems in the churches, and advice on how to live a Christian life. The letters were not originally intended to be a treatise on Christianity, but they became so over time.

When Paul returned to Jerusalem with a group of converts in the late A.D. 50s, he was arrested and imprisoned. Because he was a Roman citizen, he was sent to a prison in Rome. Roman leaders realized that Christianity had become popular. They feared this new religion posed a threat to the Roman Empire, so they made Christianity illegal. The Romans, likely in a mass execution of Christians, killed Paul in A.D. 64.

REVIEW & ASSESS

1. **Analyze Cause and Effect** What caused Paul to convert to Christianity?

_____

_____

2. **Draw Conclusions** How did Paul's epistles help spread the teachings of Jesus?

_____

_____

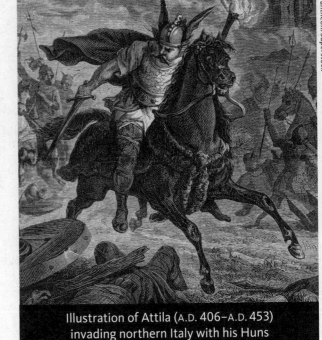

Illustration of Attila (A.D. 406–A.D. 453)
invading northern Italy with his Huns

UNIT 4 BIOGRAPHY
ATTILA

Attila, king of the Huns, was one of the most notorious of the barbarian rulers. Using cunning threats and ferocious fighting methods, Attila and the Huns attacked both the Western and Eastern Roman Empires. Though there are no records describing his qualities as a leader, some argue that his many military successes show that he was an outstanding military commander.

- **Job:** King of the Huns
- **Arch Enemies:** Romans, Visigoths
- **Talents:** Invading, Conquering

Not much is known about Attila's early life. Some believe that he was born in the area that is present-day Hungary around A.D. 406. During the fifth century, the Huns ruled a large empire. Attila ruled as king of the Huns from 434 to 453. He ruled with his brother, Bleda, until 445, when Attila murdered Bleda and became the sole ruler.

At the time of Attila's rule, the Western Roman Empire was disintegrating. Invasions by several barbarian tribes added to the instability. The Eastern Roman Empire and its capital in Constantinople were stronger and more stable. To keep from being attacked by the Huns, the Eastern emperor signed a treaty with Attila and his brother in which he agreed to pay 700 pounds of gold tribute each year.

However, when the Eastern Romans failed to keep up the payments, Attila attacked the empire in 441 and again in 443. The attacks resulted in the Eastern Roman Empire losing much of its land in southeastern Europe. Attila also demanded that the Eastern Romans pay the tribute that was owed, and then he tripled future tributes to 2,100 pounds of gold each year.

In 451, Attila turned his attention to Gaul, or present-day France. He wanted to reclaim the land that the Visigoths, one of the Germanic tribes, had conquered. In the meantime the powerful Roman general Aetius allied himself with Theodoric I, the king of the Visigoths. They combined their forces against Attila and the Huns and forced them to withdraw. This was Attila's only defeat.

Two years after that defeat, Attila planned to attack the Eastern Roman Empire. The emperor there had refused to pay the tribute that Attila demanded. However, the night before the planned attack, Attila died in his sleep.

REVIEW & ASSESS

1. **Analyze Cause and Effect** What effect did the Eastern Roman emperor's failure to pay tribute to Attila have on the Eastern Roman Empire?

   _____

   _____

2. **Make Inferences** Why do you think Attila was considered an outstanding military commander?

   _____

   _____

Pantheon/Superstock

DOCUMENT-BASED QUESTION

Use the questions here to help you analyze the sources and write your paragraph.

DOCUMENT ONE: The Parable of the Good Samaritan

1A According to this parable, how should we answer the question "Who is my neighbor?"?

_____
_____
_____

1B Constructed Response How does the Samaritan's response to the beaten man differ from the responses of the priest and Levite?

_____
_____
_____

DOCUMENT TWO: from Paul's Epistle to the Galatians

2A According to Paul, what makes all people "sons of God"?

_____
_____
_____
_____

2B Constructed Response What important Christian ideas is Paul stating in this epistle?

_____
_____
_____
_____

SYNTHESIZE & WRITE

What are some fundamental Christian ideas about how people should treat one another?

Topic Sentence: _____
_____

Your Paragraph: _____
_____
_____
_____

UNIT 4 **CHAPTER 13** SECTION 1
The Early Empire

READING AND NOTE-TAKING

IDENTIFY PROBLEMS AND ADVANTAGES As you read Section 1, use the table below to take notes on the problems and advantages faced in the Byzantine Empire following the fall of Rome.

Problems	Advantages
Open to attack	Well situated for trade

NATIONAL
GEOGRAPHIC
LEARNING

READING AND NOTE-TAKING

SEQUENCE NAME CHANGES   As you read Section 1, notice the series of name changes that affected Byzantium and the Roman Empire after the division of the Roman Empire. Keep track of these changes using the boxes below. Include details of who changed the names, when, and why.

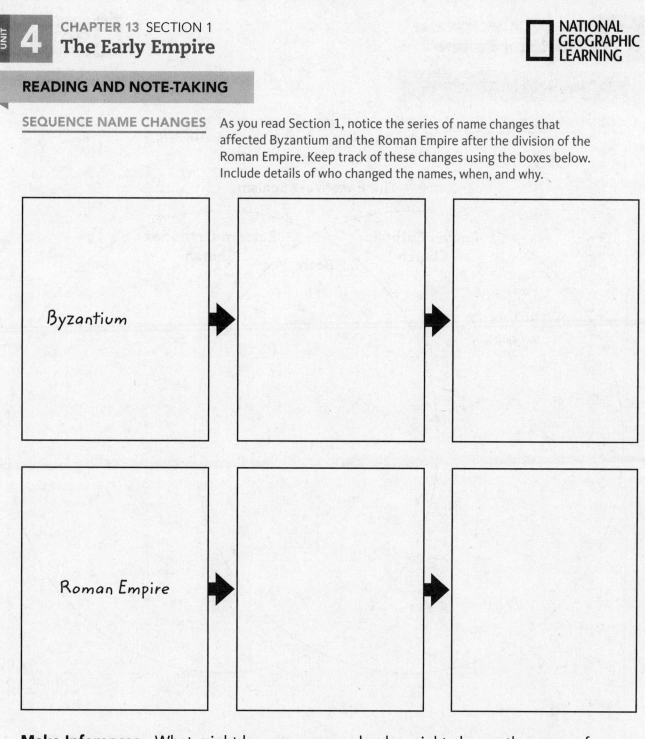

Byzantium →   →

Roman Empire →   →

Make Inferences   What might be one reason a leader might change the name of a city or an empire?

_____

_____

_____

UNIT 4

CHAPTER 13 SECTION 2
The Later Empire

READING AND NOTE-TAKING

COMPARE AND CONTRAST Use the Venn Diagram below to compare and
contrast the Roman Catholic Church and Eastern
Orthodox Church as you read Lesson 2.1.

The East-West Schism

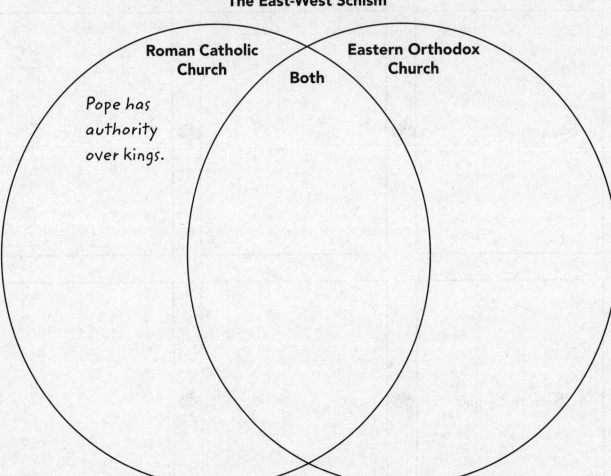

Roman Catholic
Church

Both

Eastern Orthodox
Church

Pope has
authority
over kings.

READING AND NOTE-TAKING

IDENTIFY MAIN IDEA AND DETAILS   Preview Lesson 2.3 by looking at the painting. Then complete the chart with details about the text and painting. Finally, write the main idea of the lesson in your own words.

2.3 The End of an Empire		
Interpret Visuals Based on the painting in Lesson 2.3, what do you think this lesson might be about? _____ _____		

Details: Debts and Invasions	Details: New Golden Age and Fall	Details: Painting
After Justinian's death, the plague made a comeback.		

Main Idea
_____   _____   _____

UNIT 4 | CHAPTER 13 SECTION 1
The Early Empire

NATIONAL GEOGRAPHIC LEARNING

VOCABULARY PRACTICE

KEY VOCABULARY
- **crossroads** *n.* the place where two roads meet
- **diversity** (dy-VUHR-suh-tee) *n.* a range of different things; a variety

<u>VOCABULARY Y-CHART</u> Complete a Y-Chart to compare the meanings of the vocabulary words *crossroads* and *diversity*.

Word: *crossroads*

Definition

Word: *diversity*

Definition

Similarities

UNIT 4 CHAPTER 13 SECTION 1
The Early Empire

NATIONAL GEOGRAPHIC LEARNING

VOCABULARY PRACTICE

KEY VOCABULARY

- **divine** (DEE-vyne) *adj.* having the nature of a god
- **heresy** (HAIR-uh-see) *n.* beliefs contrary to Church teachings; opposition to Church policy

DEFINITION MAP Complete a Definition Map for each Key Vocabulary word.

WORD	DEFINITION	SENTENCE
divine	EXAMPLE	

WORD	DEFINITION	SENTENCE
heresy	EXAMPLE	

UNIT 4

CHAPTER 13 SECTION 2
The Later Empire

NATIONAL
GEOGRAPHIC
LEARNING

VOCABULARY PRACTICE

KEY VOCABULARY

- **creed** *n.* a statement of belief

- **excommunicate** (ECKS-kah-myoon-uh-kate) *v.* to officially exclude a member of a church from its rituals and membership

- **icon** (EYE-kawn) *n.* an image of Jesus or a saint

- **patriarch** (PAY-tree-arkh) *n.* the leader of the Eastern Orthodox Church

- **schism** (SKIH-zuhm) *n.* a separation

TRAVEL ARTICLE   Imagine you are a travel writer traveling across Turkey and taking a tour of Hagia Sophia. Use details from Section 2 to retell the history you learned during your tour about how the church divided. Use all of the Key Vocabulary words in your article.

Article Title: _____

Date: _____

_____

_____

_____

_____

_____

_____

_____

_____

_____

_____

_____

_____

_____

_____

_____

_____

The Later Empire

NATIONAL GEOGRAPHIC LEARNING

VOCABULARY PRACTICE

KEY VOCABULARY

- **creed** *n.* a statement of belief
- **excommunicate** (ECKS-kah-myoon-uh-kate) *v.* to officially exclude a member of a church from its rituals and membership
- **icon** (EYE-kawn) *n.* an image of Jesus or a saint
- **patriarch** (PAY-tree-arkh) *n.* the leader of the Eastern Orthodox Church
- **schism** (SKIH-zuhm) *n.* a separation

THREE-COLUMN CHART Complete the chart for each of the five Key Vocabulary words. Write the word and its definition. Then provide a definition using your own words.

Word	Definition	In My Own Words

Chapter 13 SECTION 2 **ACTIVITY B** WORLD HISTORY

UNIT 4
BIOGRAPHY
THEODORA

Theodora, the empress of the Byzantine Empire, was a trusted adviser to her husband and co-ruler, Justinian I. She was also powerful in her own right and influential in much of the legislation passed during Justinian's reign.

- **Job:** Byzantine Empress
- **Characteristics:** Intelligent, Persuasive
- **Co-Ruler:** Justinian

Not much is known about Theodora's early life. She was born in A.D. 497 to a poor family. Her father was a bear keeper for a circus in Constantinople. At one point in her youth, Theodora made a living as an actress and also as a wool spinner.

Theodora's beauty and superior intelligence attracted Justinian, who married her in 525. Her strong and persuasive personality prepared her well for her role as empress. Theodora influenced nearly all the laws passed under Justinian's rule, and Justinian considered her his co-ruler. Theodora demonstrated skill in handling political affairs, including receiving and corresponding with foreign leaders—two duties previously performed only by the emperor.

Throughout his reign, Justinian sought and generally followed Theodora's advice. During the Nika riots in 532, for example, two political groups banded together to oppose the government and install their own emperor. Justinian's advisors urged him to leave. Theodora, however, counseled Justinian to stay and keep his empire

Detail of a Byzantine mosaic of Theodora (A.D. 497–A.D. 565)

Empress Theodora with her court of two ministers and seven women, detail of Theodora, c.547 A.D. (mosaic) (detail of 220592 & 244980), Byzantine School, (6th century) / San Vitale, Ravenna, Italy / Bridgeman Images

intact. Justinian took Theodora's advice. His generals then gathered the rebel groups and executed them.

Some of Theodora's most important accomplishments concerned protecting different groups in the empire. She introduced laws that enhanced women's rights, including laws that provided greater benefits for women after divorce. She also worked to protect religious freedoms in the empire, and she demonstrated charity with the poor. For these reasons, Theodora is frequently portrayed as a heroine and a champion for the less-fortunate.

When Theodora died in 548, Justinian was devastated by her death. Historians have noted that very few laws were enacted between the time of her death and Justinian's death in 565.

REVIEW & ASSESS

1. **Summarize** In what ways did Empress Theodora demonstrate her skills in politics and foreign affairs?

_____

_____

2. **Make Inferences** What does the fact that very few laws were passed after Theodora's death say about her political influence?

_____

_____

SOCIAL STUDIES SKILLS
READING AND WRITING

SOCIAL STUDIES
SKILLS | UNIT **1** | **Chapter 1: The Development of Human Societies**
READING LESSON

NATIONAL GEOGRAPHIC LEARNING

COMPARE AND CONTRAST

LEARNING THE STRATEGY

Have you ever described your home to a friend? Maybe when you have, you discovered that, while you live in a house, your friend lives in an apartment building. Both of these places share many similarities, such as walls, a roof, a door, and a kitchen, but they also have some differences. When you talk about how things are alike, you are comparing them. When you talk about how things are different, you are contrasting them.

Archaeologists frequently describe ancient cultures by comparing and contrasting them. When archaeologists **compare** cultures, they explain similarities and differences. However, when archaeologists **contrast** cultures, they present only the differences. To grasp an archaeologist's comparisons and contrasts, follow these steps.

Step 1 Determine what the subject of a passage or a paragraph is.

Step 2 In the passage, identify several specific features about the subject that are being compared and those that are being contrasted.

Step 3 Search for clue words that indicate similarities (comparing). Common clue words include *similarly*, *also*, *in addition*, and *both*.

Step 4 Search for clue words that indicate differences (contrasting). Common clue words include *in contrast*, *unlike*, *on the other hand*, and *however*.

GUIDED MODEL

(A) Prehistoric Cave Paintings
Around 35,000 years ago, an artistic explosion occurred when humans began painting detailed images on cave walls. **(B)** The subjects of these cave paintings vary quite a bit, which is not surprising since they were created over a span of 25,000 years. **(C)** The paintings often depict side-view images of animals, including woolly mammoths and horses. **(C)** Many images also feature everyday scenes, such as deer being hunted by men with spears. **(D)** Other images are different. Instead of animals, they consist of lines, circles, and geometric patterns.

(C) One type of image that appears all over the world is handprints. With this image, artists left behind the imprint of people who lived thousands of years ago

Step 1 Determine the subject.
    (A) The subject is prehistoric cave paintings.

Step 2 Identify the features being compared and contrasted.
    (B) The features being compared are the subjects of the cave paintings.

Step 3 Look for clue words that indicate similarities.
    (C) SIMILARITIES Many cave paintings depict side-view images of animals, feature everyday scenes, and show a handprint.

Step 4 Look for clue words that indicate differences.
    (D) DIFFERENCES Instead of animals, some images consist of lines, circles, and geometric patterns.

TIP A Y-Chart is a useful graphic organizer for comparing and contrasting two topics. List the unique characteristics in the branches and the shared characteristics in the straight section.

SOCIAL STUDIES SKILLS Continued

NATIONAL GEOGRAPHIC LEARNING

APPLYING THE STRATEGY

GETTING STARTED Now look at how information is compared and contrasted in Lesson 1.4, "Moving into New Environments," in Chapter 1. As you read the lesson, use the graphic organizer below to take notes on the similarities and differences between woolly mammoths and giant ground sloths. This will help you gain a deeper understanding of the challenges early humans faced when they hunted megafauna. Be sure to fill out the chart in your own words. Notice that when the text talks about megafauna in general, it is describing characteristics that both animals had in common. To get you started, one difference is filled in for you.

COOPERATIVE OPTION You may wish to work with a partner in your class to review the lesson and complete the graphic organizer.

TAKING NOTES

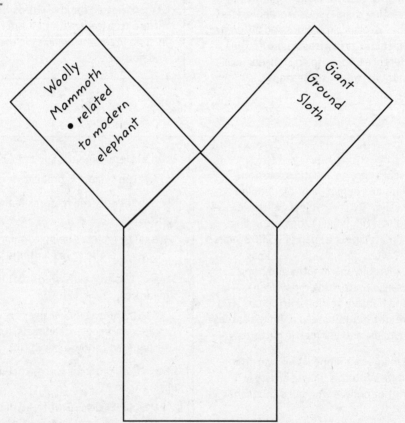

THINK AND DISCUSS

THINK ABOUT AND DISCUSS THESE QUESTIONS:

1. How were woolly mammoths and giant ground sloths similar?

2. How were woolly mammoths and giant ground sloths different?

3. After comparing and contrasting woolly mammoths and giant ground sloths, which do you think were easier for early humans to hunt?

Chapter 1: The Development of Human Societies
WRITING LESSON

WRITE AN EXPLANATION

LEARNING THE STRATEGY

When you write an **explanation**, you give readers information about a topic. You provide facts and examples so they will understand the topic more fully. To write an explanation, first select a topic. Then provide details to support your facts. The most common types of supporting details are facts, examples, statistics, quotations, expert opinions, and personal experience.

After you select your details, you need to arrange them in a logical order. If you are describing something that happened over time, it makes sense to present your details chronologically, in the order that they happened. If you're writing a how-to article, you can present the steps sequentially, one step at a time from first to last. If you are writing about a general topic, you could group your information by category.

To write an explanation, follow these steps.

Step 1 Select a topic you would like to inform your readers about and gather detailed information about it.

Step 2 Write a sentence that introduces and states your topic. This is your main idea.

Step 3 Include at least three details that provide information on your topic.

Step 4 Organize your details either chronologically, step-by-step, or by category.

Step 5 Write a concluding sentence about your topic that restates the main idea in a different way.

GUIDED MODEL

(A) Hunter-Gatherers During the Paleolithic Age
(B) For hundreds of thousands of years, people fed themselves by hunting animals and gathering wild plants to eat. **(C)** Hunter-gatherers moved with the seasons and with animal herds. They carried all of their possessions with them as they moved from place to place and built temporary homes wherever they went.

(D) Hunter-gatherers lived in groups of about 30 people and divided their tasks. Men served as the hunters. They developed tools such as spears and worked together to trap and kill their prey. Women and children usually acted as gatherers, searching for plants and preparing them to be eaten. **(E)** In their constant search for food, hunter-gatherers learned to adapt to new environments, make new tools, and build ever-warmer shelters—that's what it took to survive every day.

Step 1 Select a topic.
  (A) The topic is Paleolithic hunter-gatherers.

Step 2 Write a sentence that introduces and states your topic.
  (B) This sentence states the topic.

Step 3 Include at least three details that provide information on your topic.
  (C) The writer includes details on the topic.

Step 4 Organize your details.
  (D) The writer organizes the details by category.

Step 5 Write a concluding sentence.
  (E) The writer concludes by stating the main idea again but in a different way.

TIP Put the most exciting or interesting detail about your topic last for the most impact.

SOCIAL STUDIES SKILLS Continued

NATIONAL
GEOGRAPHIC
LEARNING

APPLYING THE STRATEGY

GETTING STARTED Now write your own explanation. In the "Write About History" section of the Chapter Review, you are asked to write a paragraph explaining how an important development of the Neolithic Age changed the way people lived during that period. Use the steps explained in this lesson and the graphic organizer below to plan your explanation. The graphic will help you clearly state your topic and organize facts about your topic into different categories. After you have organized your information, write your draft.

COOPERATIVE OPTION After you have written your draft, show it to a partner in your class and invite his or her suggestions on ways to improve the draft. You can also offer suggestions for your partner's draft. Remember to be positive and constructive.

TAKING NOTES

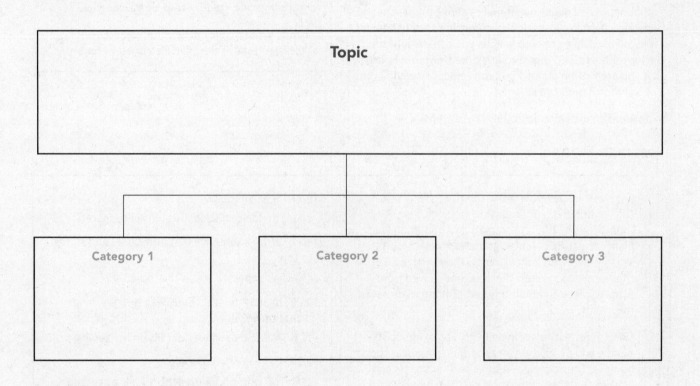

Topic

Category 1

Category 2

Category 3

THINK AND DISCUSS

AFTER YOU HAVE FINISHED WRITING YOUR EXPLANATION, THINK ABOUT AND DISCUSS THESE QUESTIONS:

1. How did you choose your topic?

2. What challenges did you face in coming up with supporting details about your topic?

3. What understanding about development in the Neolithic Age did you gain by writing the explanation?

SOCIAL STUDIES SKILLS | **UNIT 1**

Chapter 2: Origins of Civilization
READING LESSON

NATIONAL GEOGRAPHIC LEARNING

IDENTIFY MAIN IDEAS AND DETAILS

LEARNING THE STRATEGY

Have you ever read something interesting and then tried to describe it to a friend or classmate? If you recited every detail, your friend would probably get bored pretty quickly. Instead, you should tell your friend what's most important. Once your friend grasps the main idea, then you should supply a few important details about it.

The **main idea** is the most important idea in a text. Sometimes the main idea is conveyed in a sentence, but other times it may just be implied. The **supporting details** are the facts that support the main idea. If the main idea is implied, the supporting details provide clues about it. Identifying a main idea and its supporting details will help you understand a text more fully. To find the main idea and details of a paragraph, follow these steps.

Step 1 Look for the main idea in the first and last sentences of a paragraph. If the main idea is not clearly stated, look for details that give you clues about what the main idea is.

Step 2 Find the supporting details in the paragraph. These are facts, statistics, ideas, examples, quotations, and other specific items that clarify the main idea. If the main idea is in the first sentence, the supporting details follow it. If the main idea is stated in the last sentence, the supporting details come before it.

GUIDED MODEL

Çatalhöyük
(A) The people who built Çatalhöyük relied on farming for food. **(B)** A stable food supply contributed to population growth and Çatalhöyük's agriculture eventually supported as many as 10,000 people. **(B)** Farmers grew barley and wheat. They also raised livestock such as sheep, goats, and cattle for meat, milk, and clothing. **(B)** Çatalhöyük's villagers hunted and fished, too, but farming produced more food. **(B)** The surplus, or extra, food was stored for later use.

Step 1 Find the main idea in the first or last sentence.

(A) MAIN IDEA The people who built Çatalhöyük relied on farming for food.

Step 2 Find the supporting details in the paragraph.

(B) DETAIL A stable food supply contributed to population growth.

(B) DETAIL Farmers grew barley and wheat.

(B) DETAIL Farming produced more food than hunting and fishing.

(B) DETAIL The surplus food was stored for later use.

TIP When the main idea isn't stated in the first or last sentence, you have to find the implied main idea. Look at the details in the paragraph and ask yourself what they have in common. Then find the connection between them and put it in your own words. This is the implied main idea.

SOCIAL STUDIES SKILLS Continued

NATIONAL GEOGRAPHIC LEARNING

APPLYING THE STRATEGY

GETTING STARTED Now identify the main ideas and supporting details in Lesson 1.5, "North Africa: Faiyum," in Chapter 2. Read the second paragraph under "Egypt's Earliest Farming Village" and use the graphic organizer below to record its main idea and supporting details. This will help you will gain a deeper understanding of the farming practices of the Faiyum. To get you started, one supporting detail is filled in.

COOPERATIVE OPTION Fill out your own chart and then swap with a partner to compare answers. Discuss any differences you may have.

TAKING NOTES

Main Idea:

Detail
People from neighboring cultures introduced new practices.

Detail

Detail

Detail

Detail

THINK AND DISCUSS

THINK ABOUT AND DISCUSS THESE QUESTIONS:

1. Where did you find the main idea in this paragraph?

2. Where did you find the supporting details in the paragraph?

3. How do the details in the paragraph support the main idea?

Chapter 2: Origins of Civilization
WRITING LESSON

WRITE AN EXPLANATORY ESSAY

LEARNING THE STRATEGY

When you write an **explanation**, you give readers information about a topic. You provide facts and examples so they will understand the topic more fully. Suppose you want to write a three-paragraph essay. Once you have identified your topic, you would write a **thesis statement**, or main idea. This one-sentence statement explains what your essay is about. Next, you need to gather information to support your thesis statement. These details make up the body of your essay.

After you select your details, you need to arrange them in a logical order. You might present your details in the order that they happened, or chronologically; one step at a time from first to last, or sequentially; or group your information by category.

To write an explanatory essay, follow these steps.

Step 1 Select a topic you would like to inform your readers about and gather detailed information about it.

Step 2 Write a thesis statement.

Step 3 Include at least three details on your topic.

Step 4 Organize your details either chronologically, step-by-step, or by category.

Step 5 Write a concluding sentence about your topic that restates the thesis statement in a different way.

GUIDED MODEL

(A) Modern Corn and Teosinte
(B) Modern corn and teosinte are relatives and have some things in common, but they also have many differences. Teosinte was grown in ancient Mesoamerica. Modern corn developed from this earlier plant.

(C) The teosinte that was first domesticated in Mesoamerica did not look exactly like the corn we eat today. **(D)** The size of the cobs of the teosinte plant was much smaller than those of modern corn. The kernels on teosinte cobs were much harder than those on modern corn. Teosinte plants also produced many more branches on their stalks than corn today. Modern corn plants produce just a few ears of corn growing on a single stalk.

Over time, Mesoamerican farmers developed techniques that have resulted in the corn we know today. **(E)** Nevertheless, teosinte may have been smaller, more plentiful, and tougher, but we would still recognize it as corn.

Step 1: Select a topic.
  (A) The topic is modern corn and teosinte.

Step 2: Write a thesis statement.
  (B) This sentence is the thesis statement.

Step 3: Include at least three details on your topic. In this essay, details have been chosen that can be compared and contrasted.
  (C) The writer includes three details on the topic and compares and contrasts them.

Step 4: Organize your details.
  (D) The writer organizes the details by category.

Step 5: Write a concluding sentence.
  (E) The writer concludes by stating the thesis statement again but in a different way.

TIP Put the most exciting or interesting detail about your topic last for the most impact.

SOCIAL STUDIES SKILLS Continued

NATIONAL GEOGRAPHIC LEARNING

APPLYING THE STRATEGY

GETTING STARTED Now write your own explanation. In the "Write About History" section of the Chapter Review, you are asked to write a three-paragraph essay comparing and contrasting two cultures. Use the steps explained in this lesson and the graphic organizer below to plan your essay. You may want to use two graphic organizers: one to compare and contrast agricultural advances, and the other to compare and contrast technological developments. The graphics will help you organize your supporting details. After you have organized your information, write your draft.

COOPERATIVE OPTION Once you have written your draft, show it to a partner in your class and invite his or her suggestions on ways to improve the draft. You can also offer suggestions for your partner's draft. Remember to be positive and constructive.

TAKING NOTES

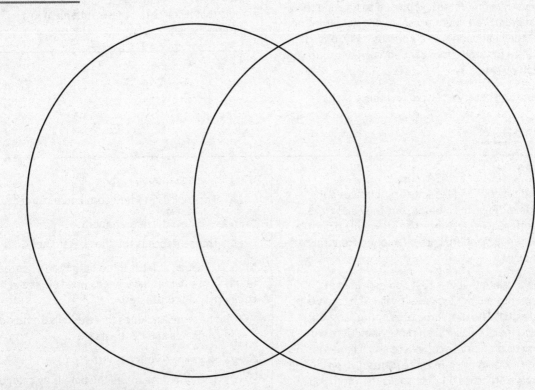

THINK AND DISCUSS

AFTER YOU HAVE FINISHED WRITING YOUR EXPLANATION, THINK ABOUT AND DISCUSS THESE QUESTIONS:

1. In which ways are the two cultures similar in terms of agricultural and technological developments?

2. In which ways are the two cultures different in terms of agricultural and technological developments?

3. How did comparing and contrasting the two cultures help you understand both of them?

SOCIAL STUDIES SKILLS | UNIT 2

Chapter 3: Ancient Mesopotamia
READING LESSON

MAKE INFERENCES

LEARNING THE STRATEGY

Think about the last time you took a nature walk through a park or other natural area. Maybe you heard the sound of birds chirping but didn't actually see them. Still, you knew that birds were making that noise because you've heard birds sing before. Perhaps you also saw prints in the dirt but noted that they weren't in the shape of a human print. You probably assumed that an animal walking through the area had made the print.

In a similar way, historians use what they know to **make inferences**, or figure out the meaning, of past events. This process helps historians analyze events. Follow these steps to make inferences and figure out the meaning of a text.

> **Step 1** Read the text looking for facts and ideas.
>
> **Step 2** Think about what the writer does not say but wants you to understand. Ask yourself: *How do these facts connect with what I already know? How does this information help me understand the text?*
>
> **Step 3** Reread the text and use what you know to make an inference.

GUIDED MODEL

The Code of Hammurabi
Hammurabi was a skillful ruler, but he is best remembered for his Code of Laws. His vast empire contained many different peoples who all followed different laws. **(A)** To help unite his empire, Hammurabi took the best existing laws, added new rules, and then organized them into a clear, written system.

(B) The Code of Laws was often applied based on a person's social class. For example, landowners could be fined more heavily than slaves. **(B)** Hammurabi also laid down detailed laws about agriculture and the buying and selling of goods.

Step 1 Identify facts stated in the text.

  FACT (A) Hammurabi organized laws into a clear system.

Step 2 Think about what the writer does not say but wants you to understand.

  UNSTATED (B) The writer doesn't explain why the Code was often based on a person's class or why it included detailed laws about agriculture and goods.

Step 3 Make an inference.

  INFERENCE Landowners could afford to pay higher penalties than people in lower classes.

  INFERENCE Agriculture and the buying and selling of goods were important elements of society.

TIP Use a three-column chart to keep track of inferences. Write down facts in the first column. Write down what you already know in the second column. Write your inferences in the third column. Note that an inference can be based on one fact or several facts.

SOCIAL STUDIES SKILLS Continued

APPLYING THE STRATEGY

GETTING STARTED Now make inferences as you read Lesson 1.2, "City-States Develop," in Chapter 3. As you read the lesson, use the graphic organizer below to take notes on the inferences you make. Making inferences about the text will help you better understand how city-states developed and were organized in Sumer. One row is filled in to help you get started.

COOPERATIVE OPTION You may wish to work with a partner in your class to review the lesson and complete the graphic organizer.

TAKING NOTES

I notice...	I know...	And so...
Most of Sumer's city-states were on the Tigris or Euphrates.	The Tigris and Euphrates were in a farming area called the Fertile Crescent.	Sumerians supported their cities by growing food on farms

THINK AND DISCUSS

THINK ABOUT AND DISCUSS THESE QUESTIONS:

1. What goods did Sumerians likely trade for tin and copper?

2. How did Sumerians pay the costs of having a government?

3. How did Sumerians use technology to maintain their power?

Chapter 3: Ancient Mesopotamia
WRITING LESSON

WRITE AN ARGUMENT

LEARNING THE STRATEGY

Suppose that you want to convince your classmates that Cyrus the Great of Persia was the most successful rule of Mesopotamia. To make your case, you would write an **argument**, which is a case that you make about an issue. You'd probably start with a summary of the issue and then state your case. This statement is called a *claim*.

To support your claim, you would provide reasons and evidence. The most common types of evidence include facts, statistics, quotations, and examples.

Finally, you have to anticipate a reader's counter-argument. Anticipating a counter-argument is called a *response*.

To write an argument, follow these steps.

Step 1 Collect information and data about your topic and decide what your claim will be.

Step 2 Write at least three reasons that support your claim. For each reason, list at least one piece of evidence that backs up the reason.

Step 3 Anticipate an argument that could be made against your claim, and write a response to that argument.

Step 4 Read your draft. Try to read it from the perspective of someone who is undecided on the issue. Then revise your argument until it as logical and persuasive as possible.

GUIDED MODEL

Why Cyrus Was the Greatest
(A) Although Akkadian emperor Sargon the Great and Chaldean emperor Nebuchadnezzar II were effective rulers, I believe that Cyrus the Great of Persia was the most successful ruler of Mesopotamia. **(B)** One reason why Cyrus was a better leader is that he showed greater tolerance to those he conquered than these rulers. Cyrus honored the people's local customs, religions, and institutions. **(B)** Cyrus also showed greater mercy to conquered peoples. Unlike Sargon and Nebuchadnezzar, Cyrus only demanded tribute the people could afford. **(B)** Cyrus set such a good leadership model that his successors followed his example. They built the largest, most stable, and most powerful empire of ancient Mesopotamia.

(C) Some might say that Sargon's rule brought such prosperity to his people that 100 years went by without widespread hunger in his empire. However, after Sargon died, his successors were unable to maintain order in the empire. As a result, the Akkadian Empire didn't last as long as the Persian Empire.

Step 1 Decide what your claim will be.

(A) The writer claims that Cyrus was the most successful ruler of Mesopotamia.

Step 2 Write at least three reasons that support your claim.

(B) The writer lists threes reasons that support the claim and backs up each one with one piece of evidence.

Step 3 Anticipate an argument.

(C) The writer anticipates an objection and responds to it.

TIP An Argument Chart can help you organize your ideas on your topic. In an Argument Chart, you list your viewpoint, or claim; your supporting details; and any opposing viewpoints that you want to respond to.

SOCIAL STUDIES SKILLS Continued

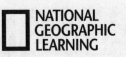
NATIONAL GEOGRAPHIC LEARNING

APPLYING THE STRATEGY

GETTING STARTED Now write your own argument. In the "Write About History" section of the Chapter Review, you are asked to identify which achievement of Mesopotamian civilizations you think has had the most important and lasting influence on the modern world and write an essay outlining your argument. Use the steps explained in this lesson and the Argument Chart below to plan your argument. Begin by filling out the chart recording your viewpoint, support, and opposing viewpoints. Then draft your essay.

COOPERATIVE OPTION Work together with a partner to complete an Argument Chart. Discuss together your claim, the details you might use to support it, and any counter-arguments others might make. Then fill out the chart and use it to write the essay.

TAKING NOTES

Viewpoint	Support	Opposing Viewpoint

THINK AND DISCUSS

AFTER YOU HAVE FINISHED WRITING YOUR ARGUMENT, THINK ABOUT AND DISCUSS THESE QUESTIONS:

1. How did you choose which reasons and evidence to use to support your claim?

2. What counter-argument did you respond to and why?

3. What understanding about the legacy of ancient Mesopotamia did you gain by writing the argument?

SOCIAL STUDIES SKILLS | UNIT 2 | Chapter 4: Ancient Egypt — READING LESSON

NATIONAL GEOGRAPHIC LEARNING

DRAW CONCLUSIONS

LEARNING THE STRATEGY

Suppose you have saved up and want to buy a new phone. Which one should you buy? You would probably read online reviews and ask your friends' opinions and use what you have learned to make an educated guess about the phone that is right for you. You make these kinds of educated guesses every day.

Historians use texts, artifacts, and other sources to **draw conclusions** about the past. Drawing conclusions about a text can help you figure out the author's purpose and point of view. It can also deepen your understanding of the text's content. Follow these steps to draw conclusions about a text.

Step 1 Read the text closely to identify the facts.

Step 2 Make educated guesses based on the facts.

Step 3 Use the educated guesses you have made to draw a conclusion.

GUIDED MODEL

Egyptian Pharaohs
Even though Egyptians did not call their kings pharaoh until after 1000 B.C., the title is generally used for all Egyptian kings. The people used the term because they were afraid to speak the king's name. **(A)** The pharaoh was worshipped as the son of Egypt's gods and a living god himself.

(A) The pharaoh's main religious role was to keep harmony by maintaining communication between Egypt's people and their gods. He was high priest of every temple and led the most important ceremonies, especially the New Year rituals to ensure bountiful harvests. With this godly role came risk. **(A)** Success reinforced the pharaoh's power. Defeat, disease, or famine threatened his authority.

Step 1 Identify facts stated in the text.

   FACT (A) Ancient Egyptians considered the pharaoh a living god. The pharaoh's main religious role was to maintain communication between the people and their gods. When he was successful, his power was reinforced. When he failed, his power was challenged.

Step 2 Make educated guesses based on the facts.

   EDUCATED GUESSES The pharaoh was worshipped when things went well. He was blamed when things didn't go well.

Step 3 Use the educated guesses you have made to draw a conclusion.

   CONCLUSION The Egyptian people believed that the pharaoh had the gods' favor when things went well. When things didn't go well, the Egyptian people believed the pharaoh had fallen out of favor with the gods and should be overthrown.

TIP Use a diagram to organize the facts you have identified and the conclusions you have made based on the facts and educated guesses. A diagram can help you clarify your thinking.

SOCIAL STUDIES SKILLS Continued

APPLYING THE STRATEGY

GETTING STARTED Now draw conclusions as you read Lesson 4.1, "Hieroglyphs and Papyrus," in Chapter 4. As you read the lesson, use the graphic organizer below to take notes on the conclusions you draw. Drawing conclusions about the text will deepen your understanding of the development of writing in Egyptian society. Study the example in the graphic organizer to help you get started.

COOPERATIVE OPTION You may wish to work with a partner in your class to review the lesson and complete the graphic organizer.

TAKING NOTES

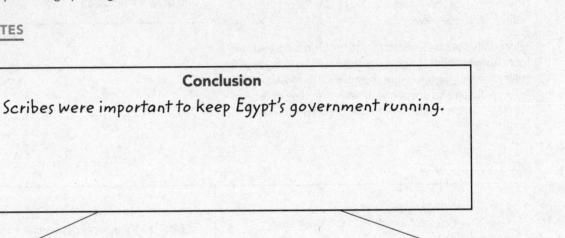

Conclusion
Scribes were important to keep Egypt's government running.

Evidence
Scribes were trained in reading, writing, law, and other fields.

Evidence
Scribes enjoyed a great deal of power and respect.

THINK AND DISCUSS

THINK ABOUT AND DISCUSS THESE QUESTIONS:

1. Why did Egyptians choose to become scribes?

2. What was especially unusual about the scribe class in Egyptian society?

3. Why was it important for scholars to crack the code of the hieroglyphics?

Chapter 4: Ancient Egypt
WRITING LESSON

NATIONAL GEOGRAPHIC LEARNING

WRITE A NARRATIVE

LEARNING THE STRATEGY

A history text usually contains **narrative** accounts of events. A narrative is an account or story of events or experiences. Narratives may be fictional, or made up, or they may be factual.

All narratives share certain characteristics, including a specific setting, or time and place. The events in a narrative usually follow a logical sequence, or order. Descriptive details, such as sensory details, help bring events and people to life. Sensory details are details that appeal to sight, sound, touch, taste, and smell.

Before writing a narrative, you should decide what point of view you will use. Most narratives are written from either a first-person or third-person point of view.

To write a historical narrative, follow these steps.

Step 1 Identify the topic of your narrative and gather facts about its events, people, and places.

Step 2 Determine the setting and point of view of your narrative.

Step 3 Recount events in a logical sequence.

Step 4 Use descriptive details to help bring your narrative to life.

GUIDED MODEL

(A) A Day in the Life of an Egyptian Trader
Life isn't always easy for a trader under Pharaoh Hatshepsut's rule, but it's never boring. **(B)** Today, for instance, we arrived in Punt. I've never seen such a land. As we pulled along the shore, we saw houses shaped like beehives rising above the water on wooden sticks. Then when we made our way onto land, we met strange-looking people with red faces and hair as long as that of our women.

(C) But the real surprises came once we arrived at the market. **(D)** As we strolled the stalls, we saw gold, wild animals, and trees that smelled sweeter than the Nile Valley after it rains. We spent all afternoon bartering our foods, wine, and other goods for these wonders.

Just before nightfall, we gathered our new luxuries for our queen and headed for the ship. **(D)** With a monkey balanced on my shoulder, I helped carry and load an entire tree in the hold. By the time we were through, I was ready for a well-earned night's rest.

Step 1 Identify the topic of your narrative.

  (A) The writer is narrating what happens in a day in the life of an Egyptian trader.

Step 2 Determine the setting and point of view of your narrative.

  (B) The narrative is set in ancient Egypt during the rule of Hatshepsut, circa 1500 B.C. The writer is using a first-person point of view.

Step 3 Recount events in a logical sequence.

  (C) The writer takes readers through the trader's day in a logical sequence.

Step 4 Use descriptive details to help bring your narrative to life.

  (D) The writer uses sensory details to describe what the trees smelled like and what the trader looked like as he carried the goods to his ship.

TIP Use an outline to help you organize the events of your narrative and write them in a logical order.

SOCIAL STUDIES SKILLS Continued

APPLYING THE STRATEGY

GETTING STARTED Now write your own narrative. In the "Write About History" section of the Chapter Review, you are asked to write a narrative describing some of the achievements of Ramses II from the perspective of a person who lived at that time. Use the steps explained in this lesson and the graphic organizer below to develop your narrative. Begin by creating an outline to plan your narrative. Write down key ideas after the roman numerals in the outline. Write down details after the letters in the outline. Be sure to choose descriptive details that help bring your narrative to life. Follow your outline as you draft your narrative.

COOPERATIVE OPTION After you have written your draft, show it to a partner in your class and invite his or her suggestions on ways to improve the draft. You can also offer suggestions for your partner's draft. Remember to be positive and constructive.

TAKING NOTES

I. _____

    A. _____

    B. _____

II. _____

    A. _____

    B. _____

III. _____

    A. _____

    B. _____

THINK AND DISCUSS

AFTER YOU HAVE FINISHED WRITING YOUR NARRATIVE, THINK ABOUT AND DISCUSS THESE QUESTIONS:

1. How did writing a first-person eyewitness account make your narrative more exciting?

2. Which details added the most important information to your narrative?

3. How did researching and writing your narrative shape your ideas about ancient Egyptian achievements?

Chapter 5: Judaism and the Israelite Kingdoms
READING LESSON

IDENTIFY MAIN IDEAS AND DETAILS

LEARNING THE STRATEGY

Think about a text you have read recently. Suppose you wanted to tell a friend about it. How would you go about it? First, you'd decide what the most important point was and describe that. Then you'd probably want to supply a few important details about the main idea.

Main ideas are in everything you read: paragraphs, passages, chapters, and books. The **main idea** is the most important idea in a text. Sometimes the main idea is a sentence or sentences, but other times it may just be implied. The supporting details are the facts that support the main idea. If the main idea is implied, the supporting details provide clues about the main idea. Being able to identify a main idea and its **supporting details** will help you understand a text more fully. To find the main idea and details of a paragraph, follow these steps.

Step 1 Look for the main idea in the first and last sentences of a paragraph. If the main idea is not clearly stated, look for details that give you clues about what the main idea is.

Step 2 Find the supporting details in the paragraph. These are facts, statistics, ideas, examples, quotations, and other specific items that clarify the main idea. If the main idea is in the first sentence, the supporting details follow it. If the main idea is stated in the last sentence, the supporting details come before it.

GUIDED MODEL

Belief in One God
(A) Belief in one God helped unify the Israelites, but their beliefs and practices also set them apart from other ancient cultures. According to the Hebrew Bible, God gave Moses a code of religious practices that governed most aspects of life. **(B)** The Israelites did not worship idols, or false gods. **(B)** They ate only certain foods. **(B)** They did not work on the Sabbath, a weekly day of rest. While they traded with other peoples, they tried to keep a distinct cultural identity. **(B)** Most Israelites did not marry outside their faith, and they were careful not to adopt foreign customs. They generally avoided the cultural diffusion, or mixing, that was a major part of many other civilizations.

Step 1 Find the main idea in the first or last sentence.

  (A) MAIN IDEA: Belief in one God united the Israelites but set them apart from other cultures.

Step 2 Find the supporting details in the paragraph.

  (B) DETAIL: Israelites did not worship idols.

  (B) DETAIL: They ate only certain foods.

  (B) DETAIL: They did not work on the Sabbath.

  (B) DETAIL: They did not marry outside the faith or adopt foreign customs.

TIP When the main idea isn't stated in the first or last sentence, you have to find the implied main idea. Look at the details in the paragraph and ask yourself what they have in common. Then find the connection between them and put it in your own words. This is the implied main idea.

SOCIAL STUDIES SKILLS Continued

NATIONAL
GEOGRAPHIC
LEARNING

APPLYING THE STRATEGY

GETTING STARTED Now identify the main idea and the supporting details in Lesson 2.3, "The Diaspora." Read the fourth paragraph under "Roman Rule" and use the graphic organizer below to record its main idea and supporting details. This will help you gain a deeper understanding of Judaism's legacy. To get you started, the main idea is filled in.

COOPERATIVE OPTION You may wish to work with a partner in your class to review the lesson and complete the graphic organizer.

TAKING NOTES

The legacy of the Jewish people is important in world history.

THINK AND DISCUSS

THINK ABOUT AND DISCUSS THESE QUESTIONS:

1. How did Judaism differ from earlier religions?

2. What religions has Judaism influenced?

3. What impact has Judaism had on Western civilization?

WORLD HISTORY **2 of 4**

Chapter 5: Judaism and the Israelite Kingdoms
WRITING LESSON

WRITE AN ARGUMENT

LEARNING THE STRATEGY

Suppose that you want to convince your classmates that monotheism is Judaism's greatest legacy. To make your case, you would write an **argument**, which is a case that you make about an issue. How would you go about making your argument? You'd probably start with a summary of the issue and then state your case. This statement is called a *claim*.

Making a claim, however, is not enough. You need to support your claim with evidence to support each of these reasons. The most common types of evidence include facts, statistics, quotations, and examples.

Finally, you have to anticipate a reader's counter-argument. Anticipating a counter-argument is called a *response*.

To write an argument, follow these steps.

Step 1 Collect information and data about your topic and decide what your claim will be.

Step 2 Write at least three reasons that support your claim. For each reason, list at least one piece of evidence that backs up the reason.

Step 3 Anticipate an argument that could be made against your claim, and write a response to that argument.

Step 4 Read your draft. Try to read it from the perspective of someone who is undecided on the issue. Then revise your argument until it is as logical and persuasive as possible.

GUIDED MODEL

Why Monotheism Is Judaism's Greatest Legacy
(A) Judaism has had an enduring impact on Western civilization, but I believe its greatest legacy is monotheism. **(B)** The worship of one God influenced religions that came later, including Christianity and Islam. **(B)** Today, these religions have the most followers in the world and exert a powerful influence in their own right. Most believers in Western society, at least, are monotheistic. **(B)** Monotheism has also influenced Western literature and culture. Many books contain references to God and describe the monotheistic life. In addition, school children in the United States are taught to pledge allegiance to their country "under God."

(C) Some might say that the Ten Commandments had a greater impact on society than monotheism. I would say that the Ten Commandments did have a big impact on society, but many of the commandments were already part of other civilizations' law systems. For example, Hammurabi's Code called for the punishment of those who stole or killed someone. Monotheism, on the other hand, was a unique idea and has had a powerful impact on the world.

Step 1 Decide what your claim will be.

  (A) The writer claims that monotheism is Judaism's greatest legacy.

Step 2 Write at least three reasons that support your claim.

  (B) The writer lists threes reasons that support the claim and backs up each one with one piece of evidence.

Step 3 Anticipate an argument.

  (C) The writer anticipates an objection and responds to it.

TIP An Argument Chart can help you organize your ideas on your topic. In an Argument Chart, you list your viewpoint, or claim; your supporting details; and any opposing viewpoints that you want to respond to.

SOCIAL STUDIES SKILLS Continued

NATIONAL
GEOGRAPHIC
LEARNING

APPLYING THE STRATEGY

GETTING STARTED Now write your own argument. In the "Write About History" section of the Chapter Review, you are asked which of the Ten Commandments you think had the greatest impact on society and list its most important effects. Use the steps explained in this lesson and the Argument Chart below to plan your list. Begin by filling out the chart recording your viewpoint, support, and opposing viewpoints. Then draft your list.

COOPERATIVE OPTION After you have written a first draft, show it to a classmate and invite him or her to provide suggestions to improve the draft. You can also offer suggestions for your partner's first draft. Be sure that your suggestions are both positive and constructive.

TAKING NOTES

Viewpoint	Support	Opposing Viewpoint

THINK AND DISCUSS

AFTER YOU HAVE FINISHED WRITING YOUR ARGUMENT, THINK ABOUT AND DISCUSS THESE QUESTIONS:

1. What was one challenge you faced when writing your list?

2. What counter-argument did you respond to and why?

3. What new understanding about the impact of monotheism on society did you gain by writing your list?

SOCIAL STUDIES SKILLS | UNIT 2

Chapter 6: Ancient India
READING LESSON

NATIONAL GEOGRAPHIC LEARNING

ANALYZE CAUSE AND EFFECT

LEARNING THE STRATEGY

Think about what happens when you bounce a ball. First, you push the ball toward the ground. The ball moves downward, strikes the ground, and then bounces back up. This series of events shows **cause and effect**. Pushing the ball is a **cause**. A cause is an event, action, or condition that makes something else happen. The action of pushing the ball causes several **effects**. An effect is an event that results from a cause.

Historians analyze cause and effect to figure out why events happened. They consider how an event led to changes over time. One cause can create several effects, or one effect may have more than one cause. A cause may be an event or an action. It may also be a condition, or a state of being. Follow these steps to figure out cause-and-effect relationships.

Step 1 Determine the cause of an event. Look for clue words that show cause, such as *because, due to, since,* and *therefore*.

Step 2 Determine the effect that results from the cause. Look for clue words such as *led to, consequently,* and *as a result*.

Step 3 Look for a chain of causes and effects. An effect may be the cause of another action or event.

GUIDED MODEL

The End of the Harappan Civilization
One of the world's earliest and most advanced civilizations was the Harappan civilization in India's Indus River Valley. The civilization began around 2500 B.C. and included some of the world's first planned cities. A combination of natural events probably contributed to its downfall. **(A)** One event was that rainfall diminished. **(A)** Another event was that earthquakes changed the course of rivers that irrigated crops. One river, the Sarasvati, no longer flowed near Harappan cities. **(B)** Because of these events, agriculture and food supplies declined.

(C) This decline led people to abandon the cities. By 1900 B.C., a simple village way of life had largely replaced the Harappans' advanced urban civilization.

Step 1 Determine the cause.
  (A) CAUSES rainfall diminished; earthquakes changed the course of rivers that irrigated crops

Step 2 Determine the effect.
  (B) EFFECT Because of these events, agriculture and food supplies declined.

Step 3 Look for a chain of causes and effects.
  (C) CAUSE/EFFECT This decline led people to abandon the cities. By 1900 B.C., a simple village way of life had largely replaced the Harappans' advanced urban civilization.

TIP Test whether events have a cause-and-effect relationship by using this construction: "Because [insert cause], [insert effect] happened." If the construction does not work, one event did not lead to the other.

SOCIAL STUDIES SKILLS Continued

NATIONAL
GEOGRAPHIC
LEARNING

APPLYING THE STRATEGY

GETTING STARTED Now practice analyzing cause and effect in Lesson 1.6, "Siddhartha and Buddhism" in Chapter 6. Use your analysis of cause and effect to deepen your understanding of the reasons why Buddhism arose in India. Use the graphic organizer below to take notes on the text. Recall that each cause you find may have more than one effect. One circle is filled in for you to help you get started.

COOPERATIVE OPTION You may wish to work with a partner in your class to review the lesson and complete the graphic organizer.

TAKING NOTES

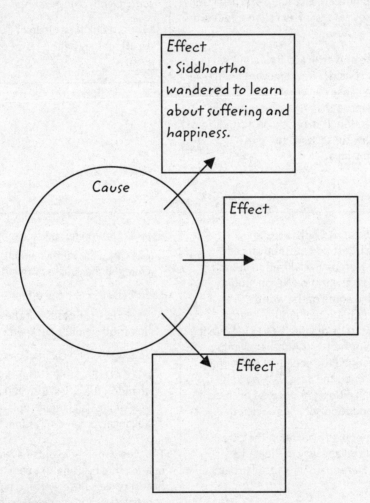

THINK AND DISCUSS

THINK ABOUT AND DISCUSS THESE QUESTIONS:

1. What was one main cause of Siddhartha's decision to seek the causes of happiness?

2. What was an immediate effect of Siddhartha's revelation?

3. How does Siddhartha's revelation continue to affect people today?

SOCIAL STUDIES SKILLS | **UNIT 2** | Chapter 6: Ancient India
WRITING LESSON

WRITE AN INFORMATIVE TEXT

LEARNING THE STRATEGY

When you write an **informative text**, you tell readers about a topic in an objective way. In other words, you inform readers without interjecting your own opinions. Suppose you want to write an informative text about games in ancient India. You could begin by introducing the topic simply—"Ancient Indians enjoyed playing games." This introduction states the main idea.

Next, include more specific information to support the main idea. For example, you might add that some of the ancient games are still popular today. You would continue to support the main idea by providing details and examples. Finally, you would end the text with a concluding sentence that summarizes or restates the main idea in a different way.

To write an informative text, follow these steps.

Step 1 Select a topic you would like to inform your readers about and gather detailed information about it.

Step 2 Write a sentence that introduces and states your topic. This is your main idea.

Step 3 Include at least three details that provide information on your topic.

Step 4 Write a conclusion that restates the main idea in a different way.

GUIDED MODEL

(A) Ancient Indian Games
(B) Ancient Indians enjoyed playing games. Some of the games they played are still popular today.
(C) You might know the game Parcheesi. In ancient India, it was called *Pachisi*. To play, opponents moved tokens on a cross-shaped board. Today, the tokens are usually made of plastic. Long ago, they were made of shells.

(C) Another ancient game was called *Chaturanga*. In this game, players used pieces representing different parts of the army. They tried to use pieces to protect the king. The game Chaturanga led to the development of chess.

(C) Historians also believe that a popular children's game was based on one played in ancient India. Players advanced toward their goal with the help of ladders, or slid backward when they encountered snakes.

(D) When people today play these games, they are enjoying the legacy of ancient India. Knowing the history of the games helps people connect with the world of long ago.

Step 1 Select a topic.
  (A) The topic is ancient Indian games.

Step 2 Write a sentence that introduces and states the main idea.
  (B) This sentence states the main idea.

Step 3 Include at least three details that provide information on your topic.
  (C) The writer includes details on the topic.

Step 4 Write a concluding sentence.
  (D) The writer concludes by stating the main idea again but in a different way.

TIP When you research, gather more information than you need. Then choose the most interesting information to include in your text.

© National Geographic Learning, Cengage Learning

SOCIAL STUDIES SKILLS Continued

NATIONAL GEOGRAPHIC LEARNING

APPLYING THE STRATEGY

GETTING STARTED Now write your own informative text. In the "Write About History" section of the Chapter Review, you are asked to write a pamphlet that informs museum visitors about the lasting influence of ancient India on religion. Use the steps explained in this lesson and the graphic organizer below to plan your informative text. The graphic organizer will help you organize your main idea and details. After you have determined your main idea and details, write your draft.

COOPERATIVE OPTION Fill out your graphic organizers independently. Then exchange graphic organizers with a partner, checking that the main idea is clear and the details support the main idea. Remember to be positive and constructive.

TAKING NOTES

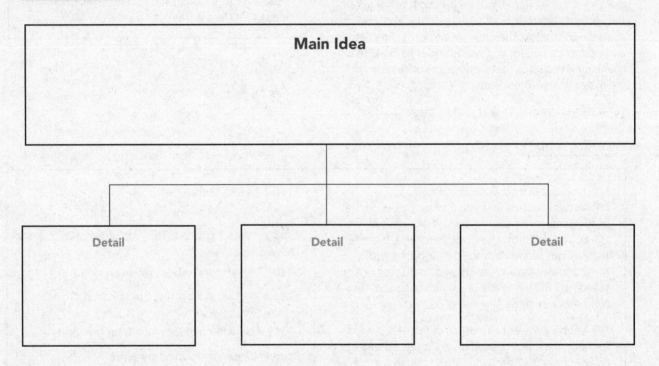

Main Idea

Detail

Detail

Detail

THINK AND DISCUSS

AFTER YOU HAVE FINISHED WRITING YOUR INFORMATIVE TEXT, THINK ABOUT AND DISCUSS THESE QUESTIONS:

1. How did you determine the main idea for your informative text?

2. What supporting details did you find were most important to use?

3. What understanding about the legacy of ancient India did you gain by writing this text?

NATIONAL GEOGRAPHIC LEARNING

ANALYZE LANGUAGE USE

LEARNING THE STRATEGY

Think of a time when you chose your words especially carefully. Perhaps you were trying to convince a friend to watch a particular movie with you. You might have decided to describe the movie as "funny" instead of "silly" to make it sound more appealing. You can often determine people's point of view on a subject by paying attention to the words they use. In a similar way, you can **analyze language use** when you read a text to note how specific word choices indicate the author's point of view and purpose.

Historians and other writers sometimes use loaded language to convey their point of view. Loaded language is wording that appeals to readers' emotions. Loaded language includes the use of words with specific connotations. A connotation is an idea or feeling a word suggests, in addition to its literal meaning. For example, a powerful king may be described either as "strong," which has a positive connotation, or as "ruthless," which has a negative connotation. Authors can also convey their point of view and purpose by including certain facts and excluding others. To analyze language use and determine an author's point of view and purpose, follow these steps.

Step 1 Identify words and phrases that have positive or negative connotations.

Step 2 Note what facts the author has included and excluded from the text.

Step 3 Determine the author's point of view and purpose.

GUIDED MODEL

(A) Shi Huangdi: A Ruthless Ruler
China's Warring States period ended when the leader of the Qin kingdom defeated all other kingdoms around 221 B.C. The leader's name was Ying Zheng, and he united the kingdoms to form an empire. He would come to call himself Shi Huangdi, meaning "first emperor."

Shi Huangdi established his government based on Legalist ideas. He set up his capital in Xianyang and built magnificent palaces in the city to demonstrate his power. **(A)** The emperor then forced thousands of China's most powerful families to relocate to the capital so he could keep an eye on them.

In addition, Shi Huangdi divided his empire into 36 areas governed by officials he himself had selected. **(A)** He also followed Legalist ideas by punishing anyone who disagreed with or criticized him. **(A)** Shi Huangdi is said to have put to death hundreds of Confucian scholars.

Step 1 Identify words and phrases that have positive or negative connotations. **(A)** Shi Huangdi is referred to as "ruthless," which suggests cruelty. He forced people to relocate to his capital and put to death those who disagreed with him.

Step 2 Note what facts the author has included and excluded from the text.

Based on what I have read here, the author includes mostly the cruel measures Shi Huangdi took and does not discuss any positive things he might have done.

Step 3 Determine the author's point of view and purpose.

I think the author sees Shi Huangdi as a cruel ruler and wants readers to share that opinion.

TIP Use a graphic organizer to note details about an author's language use as you read. After you've finished reading the text, you can use the graphic to determine the author's point of view and purpose.

SOCIAL STUDIES SKILLS Continued

NATIONAL GEOGRAPHIC LEARNING

APPLYING THE STRATEGY

GETTING STARTED Now try analyzing language use in Lesson 3.2, "Trade on the Silk Roads," in Chapter 7. As you read the lesson, use the graphic organizer below to take notes about the language the author uses. This will help you gain a better understanding of trade on the Silk Roads. To help you get started, one example of language use is filled in for you. Add more circles to the graphic organizer as needed.

COOPERATIVE OPTION Complete the graphic organizer on your own. Then exchange papers with a partner and discuss your ideas.

TAKING NOTES

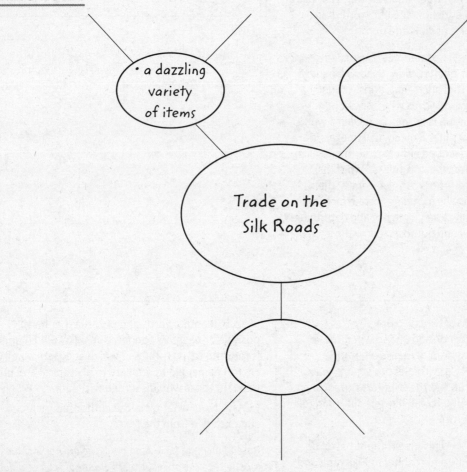

- a dazzling variety of items

Trade on the Silk Roads

THINK AND DISCUSS

THINK ABOUT AND DISCUSS THESE QUESTIONS:

1. What are some of the words the author uses to describe the goods that China traded? Do these words have mostly positive or mostly negative connotations?

2. What types of information does the author include in the lesson? What types of information is not included?

3. What do you think is the author's point of view on the Silk Roads and its trade?

SOCIAL STUDIES SKILLS | UNIT 2   Chapter 7: Ancient China
WRITING LESSON

NATIONAL GEOGRAPHIC LEARNING

WRITE AN ARGUMENT

LEARNING THE STRATEGY

Suppose that you want to convince your classmates that paper is ancient China's most important invention. To make your case, you would write an **argument**, which is a case that you make about an issue. How would you go about making your argument? You'd probably start with a summary of the issue and then state your case. This statement is called a *claim*.

Making a claim, however, is not enough. You need to support your claim with evidence, such as facts, statistics, quotations, and examples.

Finally, you have to anticipate a reader's counter-argument. Anticipating a counter-argument is called a *response*.

To write an argument, follow these steps.

Step 1 Collect information and data about your topic and decide what your claim will be.

Step 2 Write at least three reasons that support your claim. For each reason, list at least one piece of evidence that backs up the reason.

Step 3 Anticipate an argument that could be made against your claim, and write a response to that argument.

Step 4 Read your draft. Try to read it from the perspective of someone who is undecided on the issue. Then revise your argument until it is as logical and persuasive as possible.

GUIDED MODEL

Why Paper Is Ancient China's Most Important Invention
(A) The ancient Chinese made many scientific and technological contributions to world civilization, but I think China's most important invention is paper. **(B)** Paper is inexpensive and easy to use. The materials used before paper, including wood and stone, were much more costly and difficult to carve. Paper allows ideas and information to spread quickly all over the world. After the Chinese invented paper, Confucian ideas spread widely through parts of Asia. Paper also led to the development of new technologies. The printing press is a good example.

(C) Some people might say that the ancient Chinese invention of the compass was more important. They may point out that this early compass led to the development of the navigational compass, which made worldwide exploration possible. However, I think paper has had a broader use than the compass. In fact, the ancient Chinese invention of paper has been a key part of people's lives for centuries.

Step 1 Decide what your claim will be.
  (A) The writer claims that paper is ancient China's most important invention.

Step 2 Write at least three reasons that support your claim.
  (B) The writer lists threes reasons that support the claim and backs up each one with one piece of evidence.

Step 3 Anticipate an argument.
  (C) The writer anticipates an objection and responds to it.

TIP An Argument Chart can help you organize your ideas on your topic. In an Argument Chart, you list your viewpoint, or claim; your supporting details; and any opposing viewpoints that you want to respond to.

SOCIAL STUDIES SKILLS Continued

APPLYING THE STRATEGY

GETTING STARTED Now write your own argument. In the "Write About History" section of the Chapter Review, you are asked to create a list of arguments you could make about the Chinese philosophy that might be most effective as the basis for a governing policy. Use the steps explained in this lesson and the Argument Chart below to plan your list. Begin by filling out the chart recording your viewpoint, support, and opposing viewpoints. Then draft your list.

COOPERATIVE OPTION After you have written a first draft, show it to a classmate and invite him or her to provide suggestions to improve the draft. You can also offer suggestions for your partner's first draft. Be sure that your suggestions are both positive and constructive.

TAKING NOTES

Viewpoint	Support	Opposing Viewpoint

THINK AND DISCUSS

AFTER YOU HAVE FINISHED WRITING YOUR ARGUMENT, THINK ABOUT AND DISCUSS THESE QUESTIONS:

1. Which argument in your list do you think is strongest? Why?

2. How did you address one possible counter-argument?

3. What new understanding did you gain about the Chinese philosophy you chose by listing your arguments?

SOCIAL STUDIES SKILLS | UNIT 2

Chapter 8: Early Mesoamerica
READING LESSON

NATIONAL GEOGRAPHIC LEARNING

IDENTIFY MAIN IDEAS AND DETAILS

LEARNING THE STRATEGY

Have you ever watched a movie or read a book and then tried to tell a friend about it? If you recited every detail, your friend would probably get bored pretty quickly. Instead, you should figure out what's most important and tell that to your friend. Once your friend grasps the main idea, you can supply a few important details about the main idea.

Main ideas are in everything you read: paragraphs, passages, chapters, and books. The **main idea** is the most important idea in a text. Sometimes the main idea is a sentence or sentences, but other times it may just be implied. The **supporting details** are the facts that support the main idea. If the main idea is implied, the supporting details provide clues about the main idea. Being able to identify a main idea and its supporting details will help you understand a text more fully. To find the main idea and details of a paragraph, follow these steps.

Step 1 Look for the main idea in the first and last sentences of a paragraph. If the main idea is not clearly stated, look for details that give you clues about what the main idea is.

Step 2 Find the supporting details in the paragraph. These are facts, statistics, ideas, examples, quotations, and other specific items that clarify the main idea. If the main idea is in the first sentence, the supporting details follow it. If the main idea is stated in the last sentence, the supporting details come before it.

GUIDED MODEL

Maya Class System

(A) The development of Maya cities produced a class system with four main classes. **(B)** At the top was the king, who performed religious ceremonies and was believed to have descended from the gods. **(B)** Next came priests and warriors. The priests decided when farmers could plant and when people could marry. They also conducted important religious rituals and ceremonies. **(B)** Merchants and craftspeople followed the upper classes. Craftspeople made articles out of pottery and designed buildings and temples. The merchants sold and traded goods. **(B)** Finally, farmers, who made up the majority of the population, and slaves were at the bottom of the heap.

Step 1 Find the main idea in the first or last sentence.

> **(A)** MAIN IDEA: The development of Maya cities produced a class system with four main classes.

Step 2 Find the supporting details in the paragraph.

> **(B)** DETAIL: At the top was the king.

> **(B)** DETAIL: Next came priests and warriors.

> **(B)** DETAIL: Merchants and craftspeople followed the upper classes.

> **(B)** DETAIL: Farmers and slaves were at the bottom of the heap.

Tip When the main idea isn't stated in the first or last sentence, you have to find the implied main idea. Look at the details in the paragraph and ask yourself what they have in common. Then find the connection between them and put it in your own words. This is the implied main idea.

SOCIAL STUDIES SKILLS Continued

NATIONAL GEOGRAPHIC LEARNING

APPLYING THE STRATEGY

GETTING STARTED Now identify the main idea and the supporting details in Lesson 1.1, "The Geography of Mesoamerica," in Chapter 8. Read the first paragraph under "Agriculture" and use the graphic organizer below to record its main idea and supporting details. This will help you gain a deeper understanding of Mesoamerican farmers, their landscape, and the crops they grew. To get you started, one supporting detail is filled in.

COOPERATIVE OPTION You may wish to work with a partner in your class to review the lesson and complete the graphic organizer.

TAKING NOTES

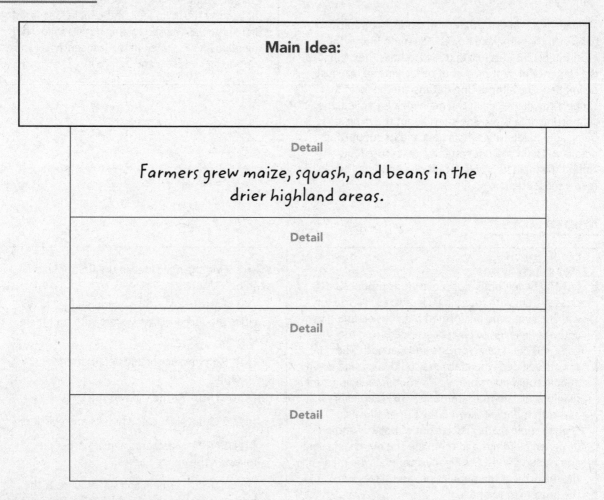

Main Idea:

Detail

Farmers grew maize, squash, and beans in the drier highland areas.

Detail

Detail

Detail

THINK AND DISCUSS

THINK ABOUT AND DISCUSS THESE QUESTIONS:

1. Where did you find the main idea in this paragraph?

2. Where did you find the supporting details in the paragraph?

3. How do the details in the paragraph support the main idea?

SOCIAL STUDIES SKILLS   **UNIT 2**

Chapter 8: Early Mesoamerica
WRITING LESSON

NATIONAL GEOGRAPHIC LEARNING

WRITE AN EXPLANATION

LEARNING THE STRATEGY

When you write an **explanation**, you give readers information about a topic. You provide facts and examples so they will understand the topic more fully. Types of explanatory writing include newspaper articles, textbooks, encyclopedia entries, and how-to articles.

To write an explanation, first select a topic. For example, suppose you want to write about the Zapotec people. You'd start by writing a sentence that introduces the topic. This is your main idea. Then you would include details that support your main idea. Next you would consider how best to organize your details. Last, you would conclude with a sentence that restates the main idea.

To write an explanation, follow these steps.

Step 1 Select a topic you would like to inform your readers about and gather detailed information about it.

Step 2 Write a sentence that introduces and states your topic. This is your main idea.

Step 3 Include at least three details that provide information on your topic.

Step 4 Organize your details either chronologically, step-by-step, or by category.

Step 5 Write a concluding sentence about your topic that restates the main idea in a different way.

GUIDED MODEL

(A) The Zapotec
(B) The Zapotec developed their own distinct and powerful civilization. **(C)** The Zapotec people would build one of the first major cities in Mesoamerica. **(C)** They developed their society in the Oaxaca Valley, a large, open area where three smaller valleys meet. **(C)** This fertile area, with its river, mild climate, and abundant rainfall, proved excellent for growing crops, especially maize. **(C)** For centuries, the Zapotec lived in farming villages located throughout the Oaxaca Valley. **(D)** Then, around 1300 B.C., a settlement called San José Magote emerged as the Zapotec center of power. Around 500 B.C., the center of power shifted when the Zapotec built a city known now as Monte Albán high atop a mountain. In time, nearly half of the Zapotec people lived in San José Magote. **(E)** With its great plazas, pyramids, and palaces, Monte Albán became the first true urban center in the Americas and a fitting symbol of the mighty Zapotec civilization.

Step 1 Select a topic.
  (A) The topic is the Zapotec.

Step 2 Write a sentence that introduces and states your topic.
  (B) This sentence states the topic.

Step 3 Include at least three details that provide information on your topic.
  (C) The writer includes details on the topic.

Step 4 Organize your details.
  (D) The writer organizes the details chronologically.

Step 5 Write a concluding sentence.
  (E) The writer concludes by stating the main idea again but in a different way.

TIP Before writing, record notes on your topic in a graphic organizer. Then select the facts, details, and examples that best develop your topic.

SOCIAL STUDIES SKILLS Continued

APPLYING THE STRATEGY

GETTING STARTED Now write your own explanation. In the "Write About History" section of the Chapter Review, you are asked to write a paragraph that explains the similarities and differences among early Mesoamerican civilizations. Use the steps explained in this lesson and the graphic organizer below to plan your explanation. The graphic will help you organize similarities and differences. After you have organized your information, write your draft.

COOPERATIVE OPTION After you have written your draft, show it to a partner in your class and invite his or her suggestions on ways to improve the draft. You can also offer suggestions for your partner's draft. Remember to be positive and constructive.

TAKING NOTES

Civilizations	Similarities	Differences
Olmec		
Zapotec		
Maya		

THINK AND DISCUSS

AFTER YOU HAVE FINISHED WRITING YOUR EXPLANATION, THINK ABOUT AND DISCUSS THESE QUESTIONS:

1. What was one challenge you faced when writing your explanation?

2. What do you consider to be the most important similarity or difference among the early Mesoamerican civilizations? What evidence from the text makes you think so?

3. What new understanding about early Mesoamerican civilizations did you gain by writing your explanatory paragraph?

SOCIAL STUDIES SKILLS | UNIT 3

Chapter 9: Ancient Greece
READING LESSON

NATIONAL GEOGRAPHIC LEARNING

COMPARE AND CONTRAST

LEARNING THE STRATEGY

When you read about history, you often compare and contrast people, events, or ideas. When you **compare** two or more things, you examine the similarities and differences between them. When you **contrast** things, you focus only on their differences.

As you read a historical text, think about the similarities and differences between the people, events, or ideas being described. Then consider how these similarities and differences deepen your understanding of the subject. For example, by comparing and contrasting the lives of men and women in ancient Athens, you will understand that they had very different experiences. To compare and contrast as you read a historical text, follow these steps.

Step 1 Determine the subject of the text that you are reading.

Step 2 In the passage, identify two or more features related to the subject that are being compared and features that are being contrasted.

Step 3 Look for comparing clue words and phrases that show how people, events, or ideas are similar, such as *both, similarly, also, too,* and *in addition to.*

Step 4 Look for contrasting clue words and phrases that show how people, events, or ideas are different, such as *unlike, in contrast, on the other hand,* and *different from.*

GUIDED MODEL

(A) Life in Athens
(B) The lives of men and women and boys and girls in ancient Athens differed greatly. **(D)** Citizenship was open to adult men who had been born in Athens. They could vote and own property. Athenian women, on the other hand, could not vote or own property. They were firmly controlled by their husbands. Women ran the household and raised children, but they could not go out alone. Poorer women had more freedom but had to work for wages.

(B) Boys and girls were also raised differently in Athens. **(C)** Like men in Athens, boys had more privileges. Boys attended school if their families could afford it. After a well-rounded education, Athenian boys went through two years of military training in preparation for citizenship. Athenian girls did not attend school, but they learned household skills at home. Poor children worked from an early age.

Step 1 Determine the subject.

  (A) The subject is life in Athens.

Step 2 Identify features being compared and contrasted.

  (B) The features being compared and contrasted are the differences for men and women and boys and girls in ancient Athens.

Step 3 Search for clue words that indicate similarities.

  (C) SIMILARITIES *Like* men in Athens, boys had more privileges.

Step 4 Look for clue words that indicate differences.

  (D) DIFFERENCES Citizenship was open to adult men who had been born in Athens. They could vote and own property. Athenian women, *on the other hand*, could not vote or own property.

Tip A T-chart is a useful graphic organizer for identifying similarities and differences about a subject. To complete a T-chart, write the topic at the top. Then write any similarities in the left column and any differences in the right column.

SOCIAL STUDIES SKILLS Continued

APPLYING THE STRATEGY

GETTING STARTED Now look at how information is compared and contrasted in Lesson 1.4, "City-States," in Chapter 9. As you read the lesson, use the graphic organizer below to take notes on the similarities and differences between Greek city-states. By identifying similarities and differences, you will develop a better understanding of the ways that Greek city-states developed. List the similarities in the left column and the differences in the right column. Be sure to fill out the chart in your own words. To get you started, one similarity is filled in for you.

COOPERATIVE OPTION You may wish to work with a partner in your class to review the lesson and complete the graphic organizer.

TAKING NOTES

Similarities	Differences
Each city had an acropolis for protection from invasion.	

THINK AND DISCUSS

THINK ABOUT AND DISCUSS THESE QUESTIONS:

1. What two features did all Greek cities have in common?

2. In what ways did Greek city-states develop differently?

3. What cultural features were shared by people who lived in different city-states?

SOCIAL STUDIES SKILLS | UNIT 3
Chapter 9: Ancient Greece
WRITING LESSON

NATIONAL GEOGRAPHIC LEARNING

WRITE AN INFORMATIVE PARAGRAPH

LEARNING THE STRATEGY

When you write an **informative paragraph**, you give readers information about a topic. You provide facts and examples so they will understand the topic more fully.

To write an informative paragraph, first select a topic and gather information on it. Then write a sentence that introduces and states your topic. This is your main idea. Back up your main idea with supporting details. The most common types of supporting details are facts, examples, statistics, quotations, expert opinions, and personal experience.

After you select the details you want to provide on your topic, you need to arrange them in a logical order. If you are describing something that happened over time, it makes sense to present your details chronologically, in the order that they happened. If you're writing a paragraph that contains instructions, you can present the steps sequentially, one step at a time from first to last. If you are writing about a general topic, you could group your information by category.

To write an explanation, follow these steps.

Step 1 Select a topic you would like to inform your readers about and gather detailed information about it.

Step 2 Write a sentence that introduces and states your topic. This is your main idea.

Step 3 Include at least three details that provide information on your topic.

Step 4 Organize your details either chronologically, step-by-step, or by category.

Step 5 Write a concluding sentence about your topic that restates the main idea in a different way.

GUIDED MODEL

(A) The Mysterious Minoans
(B) Historians know little about the Minoan civilization. **(C)** The Minoans left behind written records, but historians cannot read their language. Their knowledge of Minoan civilization is pieced together through archaeology and the writings of ancient Greek historians. **(D)** There are also many myths about this civilization. According to one myth, a king named Minos built a labyrinth beneath his palace where a terrible bull-like monster was offered sacrifices of unlucky humans. This may seem unlikely, but archaeological evidence confirms that a powerful Minoan king did build a labyrinth-like palace, and Minoans did in fact worship bulls and perform sacrifices. **(E)** Historians may know little about the Minoans, but they are discovering that information can be found in unlikely places—even in myths!

Step 1 Select a topic.
  (A) The topic is the mysterious Minoans.

Step 2 Write a sentence that introduces and states your topic.
  (B) This sentence states the topic.

Step 3 Includes at least three details that provide information on your topic.
  (C) The writer includes details on the topic.

Step 4 Organize your details.
  (D) The writer organizes the details by category.

Step 5 Write a concluding sentence.
  (E) The writer concludes by stating the main idea again but in a different way.

TIP Before writing, review the notes in your graphic organizer and select the facts, details, and examples that best develop your topic.

SOCIAL STUDIES SKILLS Continued

NATIONAL
GEOGRAPHIC
LEARNING

APPLYING THE STRATEGY

GETTING STARTED Now write your own explanation. In the "Write About History" section of the Chapter Review, you are asked to write a paragraph informing your audience about the beginnings of democracy in ancient Greece. Use the steps explained in this lesson and the graphic organizer below to plan your explanation. The graphic will help you clearly state your topic and organize your facts into different categories. After you have organized your information, write your draft.

COOPERATIVE OPTION After you have written your draft, show it to a partner in your class and invite his or her suggestions on ways to improve the draft. You can also offer suggestions for your partner's draft. Remember to be positive and constructive.

TAKING NOTES

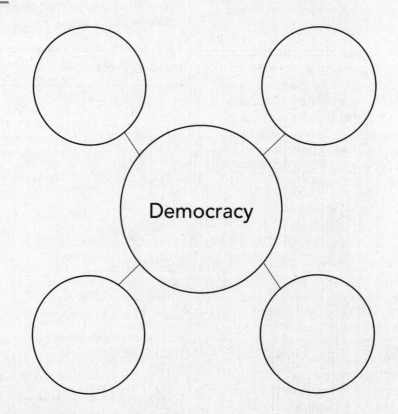

THINK AND DISCUSS

AFTER YOU HAVE FINISHED WRITING YOUR EXPLANATION, THINK ABOUT AND DISCUSS THESE QUESTIONS:

1. What was one challenge you faced when writing your explanation?

2. What information did you find most interesting about the development of democracy in ancient Greece? How did you present this information?

3. What new understanding about the development of democracy did you gain by writing your explanation?

SOCIAL STUDIES SKILLS | UNIT **3**

Chapter 10: Classical Greece
READING LESSON

NATIONAL GEOGRAPHIC LEARNING

DETERMINE WORD MEANINGS

LEARNING THE STRATEGY

When you read about history, you often come across words such as *aristocracy* or *philosophy*. Many English words are based on Greek words. For example, the word *aristocracy* uses the Greek roots *aristo-* meaning "best" and *-cracy* meaning "government." This information will help you understand that *aristocracy* means "government by those considered to be the best or most privileged people." If you know the meanings of the most common Greek roots, you can use them to determine the meanings of many words.

As you read historical texts, look for words that have Greek roots. To find each word's meaning, think of the meaning of the root and also consider the context, or the text around the word. To determine the meanings of words based on Greek roots, follow these steps.

Step 1 As you read the text, identify words with Greek roots.

Step 2 Use the meaning of the Greek roots and context clues to help you determine word meanings.

GUIDED MODEL

Cities in Ancient Greece
Ancient Greeks built their cities near coastlines and on hilltops. Location on a coastline was ideal for trade, and the hilltops helped provide a defense. Each city had a walled fortress, known as an **(A)** acropolis, **(B)** built at its highest point to protect citizens against invasion. Each city also had an open space known as an agora. The agora was used as a gathering place for citizens. People bought and sold goods, held festivals and meetings, and watched sporting events in the agora.

Greek cities were isolated from one another, so they developed separate identities despite their similarities. For example, Greek cities were governed in very different ways. Some were ruled by a **(A)** monarch who **(B)** held all of the power. Others were ruled by an **(A)** oligarchy **(B)** made up of a small but powerful merchant class.

Step 1 Identify words with Greek roots.

  (A) WORDS WITH GREEK ROOTS acropolis, monarch, oligarchy

Step 2 Determine word meanings using Greek roots and context clues.

Acropolis has the Greek roots *acr-*, meaning "top or height," and *poli-* meaning "city."

Monarch has the Greek roots *mono-*, meaning "one," and *arch-*, meaning "ruler or chief."

Oligarchy has the Greek roots *olig-*, meaning "few," and *arch-*, meaning "ruler or chief."

(B) CONTEXT CLUE An acropolis was built at a city's highest point.

A monarch was a ruler who held all of the power.

An oligarchy was made up of a small but powerful merchant class.

Tip Spend time memorizing common Greek roots and their meanings. Learning them will help you determine the meanings of many unfamiliar words in historical texts.

SOCIAL STUDIES SKILLS Continued

APPLYING THE STRATEGY

GETTING STARTED Now determine the meaning of words that have Greek roots in Lesson 4.1, "Philosophy and Literature," in Chapter 10. Becoming familiar with common Greek roots will help you gain a deeper understanding of the ideas and questions posed by Greek thinkers. Use the graphic organizer below to record examples of words with Greek roots that appear in the lesson. List those words in the first column. Identify the word's Greek root(s) in the second column and the definition of the root(s) in the third column. Then write a definition for the word in the fourth column. Use context clues to help you determine word meanings.

COOPERATIVE OPTION You may wish to work with a partner in your class to review the lesson and complete the graphic organizer.

TAKING NOTES

Word from Text	Greek Root(s)	Meaning of Root(s)	Meaning of Word

THINK AND DISCUSS

THINK ABOUT AND DISCUSS THESE QUESTIONS:

1. What two Greek roots make up the word *philosopher*? Based on the meaning of the roots, what does *philosopher* mean?

2. The word *biology* is made up of the Greek roots *bio-* meaning "life" and *-logy* meaning "study of." Based on its Greek roots, what does the word *biology* mean?

3. What Greek root makes up the word *mythical*? Based on the meaning of the root and how the word is used in the text, what does *mythical* mean?

SOCIAL STUDIES SKILLS | UNIT 3

Chapter 10: Classical Greece
WRITING LESSON

NATIONAL GEOGRAPHIC LEARNING

WRITE AN INFORMATIVE TEXT

LEARNING THE STRATEGY

When you write an **informative text,** you tell readers about a topic in an objective and factual way. In other words, you inform readers without interjecting your own opinions. Informative text conveys ideas accurately and without bias.

For example, suppose you are assigned to write an informative text that tells readers about the role Greek gods played in ancient Greece. You might begin by introducing the topic simply and clearly with your main idea: "Greek gods played an important role in ancient Greece." As you continue writing your informative text, you will want to include more specific information to support the main idea by providing more details and examples. To sum up your informative text and to remind readers of the main idea, you should end with a concluding sentence that summarizes or restates the main idea in a different way.

To write an informative text, follow these steps.

Step 1 Select a topic you would like to inform your readers about and gather detailed information about it.

Step 2 Write a sentence that introduces and states your topic. This is your main idea.

Step 3 Include at least three details that provide information on your topic.

Step 4 Write a conclusion that summarizes your topic and restates the main idea.

GUIDED MODEL

(A) The Role of Greek Gods
(B) Greek gods played an important role in ancient Greece. **(C)** The Greeks believed that unhappy gods showed their displeasure by causing problems in people's lives. As a result, people tried to obtain the gods' help by leaving offerings outside temples.

(C) The Greek people also observed a holy day for each god and goddess. These special days involved great processions, offerings, poetry recitals, and competitive sports, including the original Olympic Games. **(C)** For private worship, most Greek homes had small altars where people would pray to the gods.

(D) Greek gods played an important role in ancient Greece. The ancient Greeks believed that the gods influenced daily life. Keeping the gods happy involved worship, sacrifice, and celebration.

Step 1 Select a topic.
  (A) The topic is the role of Greek gods.

Step 2 Introduce your topic by stating the main idea.
  (B) This sentence states the topic.

Step 3 Include details that provide information on your topic.
  (C) The writer includes details on the topic.

Step 4 Conclude by summarizing and restating the main idea.
  (D) The writer concludes by stating the main idea again but in a different way.

TIP Make sure your conclusion briefly summarizes the most important points.

SOCIAL STUDIES SKILLS Continued

APPLYING THE STRATEGY

GETTING STARTED Now write your own informative text. In the "Write About History" section of the Chapter Review, you are asked to write a speech that informs new American citizens about how the democratic concepts developed in Greece laid the foundation for democracy in the United States. Use the steps explained in this lesson and the graphic organizer below to plan your informative speech. The graphic will help you organize your main idea and details. After you have determined your main idea and details, write your draft.

COOPERATIVE OPTION After you have written your draft, show it to a classmate and invite him or her to provide suggestions to improve the draft. You can also offer suggestions for your partner's draft. Remember to be positive and constructive.

TAKING NOTES

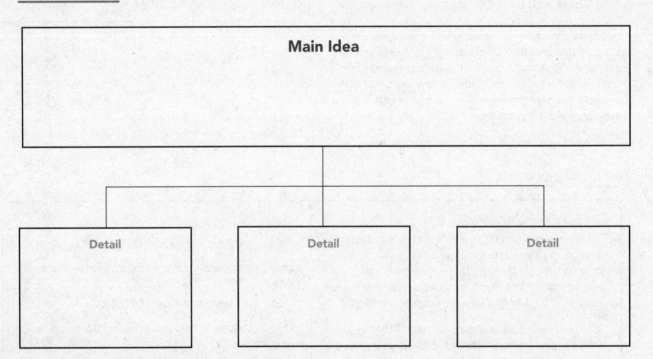

THINK AND DISCUSS

AFTER YOU HAVE FINISHED WRITING YOUR INFORMATIVE SPEECH, THINK ABOUT AND DISCUSS THESE QUESTIONS:

1. What was one challenge you faced when writing your informative speech?

2. What information did you find most interesting about Pericles and his influence on democratic ideas in ancient Greece? How did you present this information in your speech?

3. What new understanding about democracy in the United States did you gain by writing your informative speech?

Chapter 11: The Roman Republic
READING LESSON

COMPARE AND CONTRAST

LEARNING THE STRATEGY

Have you ever described a t-shirt by comparing and contrasting it with another? You might point out that a t-shirt that advertises a movie has a crew neck and short sleeves like any other t-shirt. However, it differs from other t-shirts because it shows a design or line from the film. When you talk about how things are alike, you are comparing them. When you talk about how things are different, you are contrasting them.

Historians often describe past events and situations by comparing and contrasting them. When historians **compare** what happened in the past, they explain similarities and differences. When historians **contrast** what happened in the past, they present only the differences. To grasp a historian's comparisons and contrasts, follow these steps.

Step 1 Determine what the subject of a passage or a paragraph is.

Step 2 In the passage, identify several specific features about the subject that are being compared and those that are being contrasted.

Step 3 Search for clue words that indicate similarities (comparing). Common clue words include *similarly, also, in addition*, and *both*.

Step 4 Search for clue words that indicate differences (contrasting). Common clue words include *in contrast, unlike, on the other hand*, and *however*.

GUIDED MODEL

(A) Slaves in the Roman Republic
(B) Slaves were the largest class in Rome. **(C)** Most slaves were bought from foreign traders. **(D)** However, some slaves were prisoners from Rome's conquests.

(B) Slaves were very useful in Rome's economy. **(C)** Most worked at manual labor, from household chores to construction work or agriculture. **(D)** However, skilled slaves might be craftspeople, and educated slaves might be teachers, doctors, or managers of their master's business.

(B) The treatment of slaves varied. **(C)** Many slaves were treated well. **(D)** Still, others suffered very badly. Excessive punishments could spark rebellion. A slave named Spartacus led the most famous rebellion in 73 B.C. For about two years, his slave army fought the Roman soldiers and controlled large areas of the countryside.

Step 1 Determine the subject.

   (A) The subject is Roman slaves.

Step 2 Identify the features being compared and contrasted.

   (B) The features being compared are who made up the slave class, how slaves were employed, and how slaves were treated.

Step 3 Look for word clues that indicate similarities.

   (C) SIMILARITIES Most slaves were bought from foreign traders, performed manual labor, and were treated well.

Step 4 Look for clue words that indicate differences.

   (D) DIFFERENCES Some slaves were prisoners of war, had better jobs, and suffered very badly.

TIP A Venn diagram is a useful graphic organizer for comparing and contrasting two topics. In a Venn diagram, list unique characteristics in the left and right sides and common characteristics in the overlapping area.

SOCIAL STUDIES SKILLS Continued

NATIONAL GEOGRAPHIC LEARNING

APPLYING THE STRATEGY

GETTING STARTED Now describe how information is presented comparatively in Lesson 2.1, "Men and Women," in Chapter 11. As you read, use the graphic organizer below to take notes on the similarities and differences between men and women in the Roman Republic. This will help you gain a deeper understanding of Roman daily life. Be sure to fill out the chart in your own words. Remember to look for signal words like *most*, *however*, and *still*. To get you started, one difference is filled in for you.

COOPERATIVE OPTION You may wish to work with a partner in your class to review the lesson and complete the graphic organizer.

TAKING NOTES

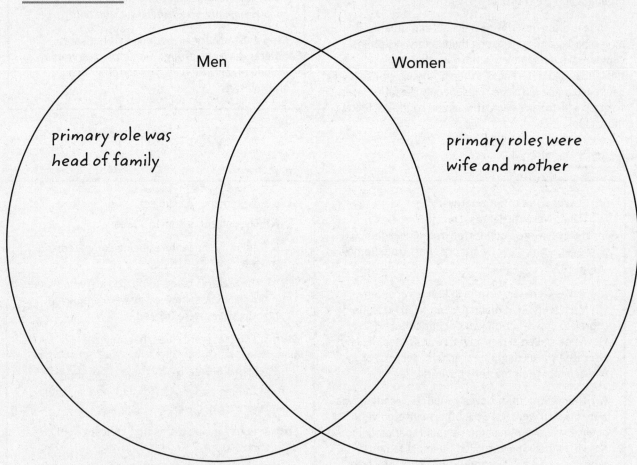

Men

Women

primary role was head of family

primary roles were wife and mother

THINK AND DISCUSS

THINK ABOUT AND DISCUSS THESE QUESTIONS:

1. How did the education of boys and girls differ in ancient Rome?

2. How did the roles of men and women in families differ?

3. In what ways were men's and women's roles in business similar?

SOCIAL STUDIES SKILLS | **UNIT 4**
Chapter 11: The Roman Republic
WRITING LESSON

NATIONAL GEOGRAPHIC LEARNING

WRITE AN ARGUMENT

LEARNING THE STRATEGY

Suppose that you want to convince your classmates that Pericles was the greatest leader of ancient Athens. To make your case, you would write an **argument**, which is a case that you make about an issue. How would you go about making your argument? You'd probably start with a summary of the issue and then state your case. You would say something like, "Ancient Athens had many great leaders, but I believe that Athens's greatest leader was Pericles." This statement is called a *claim*.

However, the claim alone isn't enough. You have to provide support for the claim by giving reasons and evidence. The most common types of evidence include facts, statistics, quotations, and examples.

Finally, you have to anticipate a reader's counter-argument. Anticipating a counter-argument is called a *response*.

To write an argument, follow these steps.

STEPS IN WRITING AN ARGUMENT

Step 1 Collect information and data about your topic and make a T-Chart that lists pros and cons—arguments on each side of the issue. Then decide what your claim will be.

Step 2 Write at least three reasons that support your claim. For each reason, list at least one piece of evidence that backs up the reason.

Step 3 Anticipate an argument that could be made against your claim, and write a response to that argument.

Step 4 Read your draft. Try to read it from the perspective of someone who is undecided on the issue. Then revise your argument until it as logical and persuasive as possible.

GUIDED MODEL

Why Pericles Was a Great Leader
(A) Ancient Athens had many great leaders, but I believe that Athens's greatest leader was Pericles.
(B) One reason why Pericles was such a good leader was that he expanded democracy. He led the Assembly in passing laws that allowed more citizens to vote. **(B)** Another reason why Pericles was so effective was that he made the military of Athens stronger. For example, he built up Athens's navy. **(B)** Finally, Pericles beautified Athens by constructing buildings such as the Parthenon.

(C) Some might say that Pericles didn't expand democracy enough because women could not be citizens or vote. At that time, though, women didn't have rights in any part of the world. For that time, Pericles went further than any other ruler in giving people a voice in government.

Step 1 Decide what your claim will be.
  (A) The writer claims that Pericles was Athens' greatest leader.

Step 2 Write at least three reasons that support your claim.
  (B) The writer lists threes reasons that support the claim and backs up each one with one piece of evidence.

Step 3 Anticipate an argument.
  (C) The writer anticipates an objection and responds to it.

TIP A T-chart is a useful graphic organizer for planning your argument. It helps you understand both sides of an issue. In the left column, list arguments on one side of an issue. On the right side, list arguments on the other side.

SOCIAL STUDIES SKILLS Continued

NATIONAL
GEOGRAPHIC
LEARNING

APPLYING THE STRATEGY

GETTING STARTED Now write your own argument. In the "Write About History" section of the Chapter Review, you are asked to outline the points you'd make in an argument either favoring Julius Caesar's assassination or opposing it. Use the steps explained in this lesson and the T-chart below to plan your argument. Begin by filling out the chart listing both sides of the issue. Then draft your argument.

COOPERATIVE OPTION After you have written your draft, show it to a partner in your class and invite his or her suggestions on ways to improve the draft. You can also offer suggestions for your partner's draft. Remember to be positive and constructive.

TAKING NOTES

T-Chart of Pros and Cons	
Pros—Arguments on One Side of the Issue	**Cons—Arguments on the Other Side of the Issue**
Claim:	

THINK AND DISCUSS

AFTER YOU HAVE FINISHED WRITING YOUR ARGUMENT, THINK ABOUT AND DISCUSS THESE QUESTIONS:

1. What was one of the challenges you faced in writing your argument?

2. How did you answer an objection that an opponent might have?

3. What understanding about Rome did you gain by writing the argument?

SOCIAL STUDIES SKILLS — UNIT 4

Chapter 12: The Roman Empire and Christianity
READING LESSON

NATIONAL GEOGRAPHIC LEARNING

SEQUENCE EVENTS

LEARNING THE STRATEGY

When you tell your friends the plot of a movie you've just seen, you probably describe its events in the order they occurred. You start at the beginning and continue to the end. When you relate events in the order in which they occurred in time, you **sequence events**. Thinking about events in time order helps you understand how they relate to each other.

Historians often sequence events to tell how a civilization developed or describe the reign of a ruler. Identifying the time order of historic events can help you understand how the events are related. Follow these steps to sequence events.

Step 1 Look for clue words and phrases that suggest time order. Clue words include the names of months and days or words such as *before, after, finally, a year later,* or *lasted.*

Step 2 Look for dates in the text and match them to events.

GUIDED MODEL

The Destruction of Pompeii
Before the afternoon of **(B)** August 24, A.D. 79, Pompeii was an average city resting in the shadow of Mount Vesuvius, a volcano on Italy's western coast. Some 20,000 people worked, played, ate, slept, and lived within Pompeii's city walls.

(A) And then, a violent explosion brought the city to a standstill. Mount Vesuvius erupted, shooting gas mixed with rock and ash high into the sky and creating an immense black cloud that blocked out the sun. Panic-stricken citizens fled as ash rained down.

As lava crept toward the city, fires raged and buildings collapsed. A vast volcanic ash cloud swept in to suffocate the city, burying its people and their possessions nearly 25 feet deep. A cloud of poisonous gas overtook and killed anyone who had not yet escaped. **(A)** Over the next few days, lightning, earthquakes, and tidal waves followed. **(A)** Finally after three days, Vesuvius went quiet—as silent as the deserted city of Pompeii.

Step 1 Look for clue words and phrases that suggest time order.

    Time Clues (A) and then; over the next few days; finally

Step 2 Look for specific dates in the text.

    Be sure to read the text carefully. Historians may not always list the dates in time order. As you read, it is important to match the event with its date.

    Sample Date (B) August 24, A.D. 79, when Mount Vesuvius erupted and destroyed Pompeii

TIP As you read, you can create a time line to track the time order of the events discussed in the text. A time line is a visual tool that is used to sequence events. Time lines often read from left to right, listing events from the earliest to the latest.

SOCIAL STUDIES SKILLS Continued

APPLYING THE STRATEGY

GETTING STARTED Now sequence events as you read Lesson 2.4, "The Early Christian Church," in Chapter 12. Sequencing events will help you better understand the development of the early Christian Church. As you read the lesson, use the graphic organizer below to sequence events. List the earliest event in the first box on the left and the latest event in the last box on the right. Remember to use both clue words and dates to determine the time order of events. The first box is filled in to help you get started.

COOPERATIVE OPTION You may wish to work with a partner in your class to review the lesson and complete the graphic organizer.

TAKING NOTES

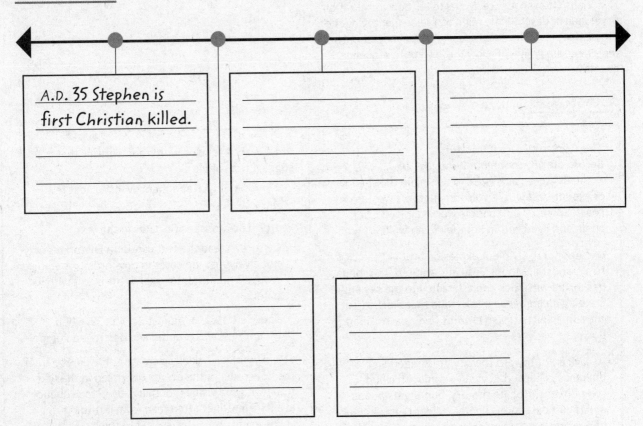

A.D. 35 Stephen is first Christian killed.

THINK AND DISCUSS

THINK ABOUT AND DISCUSS THESE QUESTIONS:

1. What event led to the deaths of thousands of Christians in Rome? When did this event occur?

2. Who ended Christian persecution, and when did this happen?

3. Put these events in chronological order: Christianity becomes Rome's official religion; the apostle Peter dies; Christian leaders meet to define Christian beliefs.

Chapter 12: The Roman Empire and Christianity
WRITING LESSON

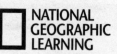

WRITE AN EXPLANATION

LEARNING THE STRATEGY

When you write an **explanation**, you give readers information about a topic. You provide facts and examples so they will understand the topic more fully. To write an explanation, first select a topic. Write a sentence that introduces and states your topic. This is your main idea. Then gather information and provide details to support your what you find. The most common types of supporting details are facts, examples, statistics, quotations, expert opinions, and personal experience.

After you select the details you want to provide on your topic, you need to arrange them in a logical order. You may present your details chronologically, sequentially, or by category.

To write an explanation, follow these steps.

> **Step 1** Select a topic you would like to inform your readers about and gather detailed information about it.
>
> **Step 2** Write a sentence that introduces and states your topic. This is your main idea.
>
> **Step 3** Include at least three details that provide information on your topic.
>
> **Step 4** Organize your details either chronologically, step-by-step, or by category.
>
> **Step 5** Write a concluding sentence about your topic that restates the main idea in a different way.

GUIDED MODEL

(A) Augustus and the Pax Romana
(B) When Augustus became the sole ruler of Rome, he made wise decisions that formed the foundation for the Pax Romana. **(C)** For example, Augustus helped prevent unrest within the empire by guaranteeing free grain to the poor. He also began a cultural revival in the city of Rome and encouraged Romans to pursue art, literature, and education. By making Rome more beautiful, Augustus encouraged Romans to take greater pride in their capital.

(D) Augustus also reformed the military. He decreased the size of the military and granted land to any soldiers who lost their jobs. By establishing these reforms, Augustus removed the army as a threat to his power and created a more stable government. **(E)** The decisions Augustus made while emperor of Rome contributed greatly to the peace and prosperity that Romans enjoyed during and after his rule.

Step 1 Select a topic.
  (A) The topic is Augustus and the Pax Romana.

Step 2 Write a sentence that introduces and states your topic.
  (B) This sentence states the topic.

Step 3 Include at least three details that provide information on your topic.
  (C) The writer includes details on the topic.

Step 4 Organize your details.
  (D) The writer organizes the details by category.

Step 5 Write a concluding sentence.
  (E) The writer concludes by stating the main idea again but in a different way.

TIP Use a graphic organizer to list your topic, introduction, ideas, details, and conclusion. You can use the graphic as a road map for your explanatory text.

SOCIAL STUDIES SKILLS Continued

APPLYING THE STRATEGY

GETTING STARTED Now write your own explanation. In the "Write About History" section of the Chapter Review, you are asked to write a speech that explains three of the problems that contributed to the decline and fall of the Roman Empire. Use the steps explained in this lesson and the graphic organizer below to plan your speech. The graphic will help you clearly state your topic and organize facts about your topic into different categories. After you have organized your information, write your draft.

COOPERATIVE OPTION After you have written your draft, show it to a partner in your class and invite his or her suggestions on ways to improve the draft. You can also offer suggestions for your partner's draft. Remember to be positive and constructive.

TAKING NOTES

TOPIC: _____

INTRODUCTION: _____
_____
_____

FACTS:

DETAILS: _____ _____ _____ _____
_____ _____ _____ _____
_____ _____ _____ _____
_____ _____ _____ _____
_____ _____ _____ _____

CONCLUSION: _____
_____
_____

THINK AND DISCUSS

AFTER YOU HAVE FINISHED WRITING YOUR SPEECH, THINK ABOUT AND DISCUSS THESE QUESTIONS:

1. What was the greatest challenge you faced as you wrote your speech?

2. What do you consider to be the most important reason for the decline and fall of Rome? What evidence from the text makes you think so?

3. What new understanding about the decline and fall of Rome did you gain by writing your speech?

Chapter 13: The Byzantine Empire
READING LESSON

ANALYZE CAUSE AND EFFECT

LEARNING THE STRATEGY

Have you ever told a story about something that happened to you? In many stories, there's an event or action that causes something else to happen. For instance, you might say, "Because the road was slippery, our car slid into a ditch." A **cause** is an event or action that makes something else happen. An **effect** is an event that happens as a result of a cause. In this example, the cause is the slippery road; the effect is sliding into a ditch.

Historians analyze cause-and-effect relationships to figure out why events happened. They consider how an event led to changes over time. One cause can create several effects, or one effect may have more than one cause. A cause may be an event or an action. It may also be a condition, or a state of being. Follow these steps to figure out cause-and-effect relationships.

Step 1 Determine the cause(s) of an event. Look for signal words, such as *because, due to, since, so,* and *therefore.*

Step 2 Determine the effect(s) of an event. Look for signal words such as *led to, consequently,* and *as a result.*

GUIDED MODEL

The City of Constantinople
(A) Due to its strategic location on the Bosporus, **(B)** Constantinople was the richest and most influential city of its time. **(B)** Merchants and traders from many parts of Europe and Asia brought in a constant flow of business and goods. **(A)** Because it was a center of trade, **(B)** Constantinople was also a center of cultural diversity. People who came from abroad to trade sometimes settled in the city.

In spite of the city's wealth, **(A)** many of Constantinople's residents lived in poor conditions. **(B)** As a result, they relied on government handouts of bread. Just a short walk away, though, spectacular public buildings and magnificent monuments inspired civic pride.

Step 1 Determine the cause(s).

  (A) CAUSE Constantinople was strategically located on the Bosporus.

  (A) CAUSE Constantinople was a center of trade.

  (A) CAUSE Many of Constantinople's residents lived in poor conditions.

Step 2 Determine the effect(s) of an event.

  (B) EFFECT Constantinople was a rich and influential city.

  (B) EFFECT Merchants and traders brought a constant flow of business and goods.

  (B) EFFECT Constantinople was a center of cultural diversity.

  (B) EFFECT Many residents relied on government handouts of bread.

TIP Test whether events have a cause-and-effect relationship by using this construction: "Because [insert cause], [insert effect] happened." If the construction does not work, one event did not lead to the other.

1 of 4 WORLD HISTORY

© National Geographic Learning, Cengage Learning

SOCIAL STUDIES SKILLS Continued

NATIONAL GEOGRAPHIC LEARNING

APPLYING THE STRATEGY

GETTING STARTED Now practice analyzing cause and effect in Lesson 2.1, "The Church Divides," in Chapter 13. By examining the causes and effects of the East-West Schism, you will come to a greater understanding of this event. Use the graphic organizer below to take notes on causes and effects in the text. Recall that each cause you find may have more than one effect. To help get you started, one cause and one effect have been filled in for you.

COOPERATIVE OPTION Fill out your cause-and-effect chart and then exchange charts with a partner to compare answers. Discuss any differences you may have.

TAKING NOTES

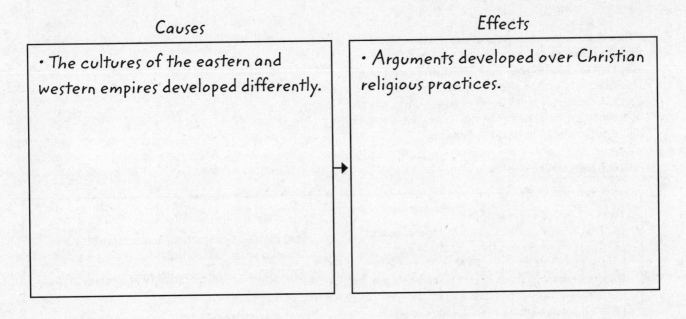

Causes
- The cultures of the eastern and western empires developed differently.

Effects
- Arguments developed over Christian religious practices.

THINK AND DISCUSS

THINK ABOUT AND DISCUSS THESE QUESTIONS:

1. What caused a power struggle between the pope in Rome and Byzantine emperors?

2. Why did the Byzantine patriarch excommunicate the pope?

3. How does examining the causes and effects of the East-West Schism help you understanding this event?

SOCIAL STUDIES SKILLS | **UNIT 4**

Chapter 13: The Byzantine Empire
WRITING LESSON

NATIONAL GEOGRAPHIC LEARNING

WRITE AN EXPLANATION

LEARNING THE STRATEGY

When you write an **explanation**, you give readers information about a topic. You provide facts and examples so they will understand the topic more fully. Types of explanatory writing include newspaper articles, textbooks, encyclopedia entries, and how-to-articles.

To write an explanation, first select a topic. For example, suppose you wanted to write about Byzantine mosaics. You'd start by writing a sentence that introduces the topic. This is your main idea. Then you would include details that support your main idea. Next you would consider how best to organize your details. Last, you would conclude with a sentence that restates the main idea.

To write an explanation, follow these steps.

Step 1 Select a topic you would like to inform your readers about and gather detailed information about it.

Step 2 Write a sentence that introduces and states your topic. This is your main idea.

Step 3 Include at least three details that provide information on your topic.

Step 4 Write a concluding sentence about your topic that restates the main idea in a different way.

GUIDED MODEL

(A) BYZANTINE MOSAICS
(B) The Byzantine Empire developed an influential artistic culture, and its distinctive style is well represented by remarkable mosaics. Byzantine mosaics depicted vibrant, detailed scenes that covered entire walls and ceilings.

(C) To make a mosaic, an artist would spread a layer of plaster onto a surface and set the cubes of stone into the wet plaster. Then to create a sparkling effect, some mosaic pieces were made of gold leaf sandwiched in clear glass. **(C)** These pieces were angled precisely to reflect light in different directions. **(C)** Finally, to create highly detailed and realistic pictures of people and animals, Byzantine mosaic artists used many different colors of stone.

(D) Byzantine mosaics stood out for their exceptional quality and craftsmanship. The breathtaking results still awe viewers today.

Step 1 Select a topic.
  (A) The topic is Byzantine mosaics.

Step 2 Write a sentence that introduces and states your topic.
  (B) This sentence states the topic.

Step 3 Include at least three details that provide information on your topic.
  (C) The writer includes details on the topic.

Step 4 Write a conclusion.
  (D) The writer concludes by stating the main idea again but in a different way.

TIP Think about the best way to organize your details for your readers. Determine what makes the most sense for your topic. You could organize information chronologically, in numbered steps, or in categories.

Name ___ Class ___ Date ___

SOCIAL STUDIES SKILLS Continued

APPLYING THE STRATEGY

GETTING STARTED Now write your own explanation. In the "Write About History" section of the Chapter Review, you are asked to suppose you are a citizen of the Byzantine Empire and write an explanation to your fellow citizens about how Theodora influenced Justinian's rule. Use the steps explained in this lesson and the graphic organizer below to plan your writing. Begin by filling in your main idea. Then come up with three details that explain the ways in which Theodora influenced Justinian's rule. After you have organized your information, write your draft.

COOPERATIVE OPTION After you have written a first draft, show it to a partner in your class and invite his or her suggestions to improve the draft. You can also offer suggestions for your partner's first draft. Remember to be positive and constructive.

TAKING NOTES

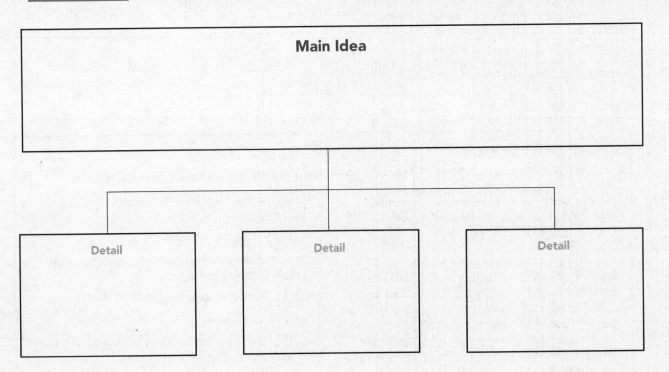

THINK AND DISCUSS

AFTER YOU HAVE FINISHED WRITING YOUR EXPLANATION, THINK ABOUT AND DISCUSS THESE QUESTIONS:

1. What do you think is the most important way in which Theodora influenced Justinian?

2. What challenges did you face while writing your explanation?

3. What understanding about Theodora and Justinian's relationship did you gain by writing the explanation?

© National Geographic Learning, Cengage Learning

WORLD HISTORY 4 of 4